The Torchlight List

The Torchlight List

AROUND THE WORLD IN 200 BOOKS

JIM FLYNN

A Herman Graf Book
Skyhorse Publishing

Skyhorse Publishing books may be purchased in bulk at special discounts for sales promotion, corporate gifts, fund-raising, or educational purposes. Special editions can also be created to specifications. For details, contact the Special Sales Department, Skyhorse Publishing, 307 West 36th Street, 11th Floor, New York, NY 10018 or info@skyhorsepublishing.com.

Skyhorse® and Skyhorse Publishing® are registered trademarks of Skyhorse Publishing, Inc.®, a Delaware corporation.

www.skyhorsepublishing.com

10 9 8 7 6 5 4 3 2 1

Library of Congress Cataloging-in-Publication Data is available on file.

ISBN: 978-1-62636-092-1

Printed in the United States of America

To my father

Joseph Roy Flynn

(1885–1955)

"You can live in the most democratic country on earth, and if you are lazy, obtuse, or servile within yourself, you are not free."
IGNAZIO SILONE, 1955

To this list should be added *"and if you do not love reading."*

CONTENTS

BORN INTO THE MAGIC REALM

My father was Joseph Roy Flynn, born in 1885, one of seven children who survived to maturity. Like most Irish-American families of the day, he and his four brothers all went into factory work between the ages of eleven and fourteen, so none of them got a high-school education. My grandfather was too proud to put his daughters into Anglo-Saxon homes as servants, so Aunt Marie and Aunt Lucy did finish high school.

My father's first job was in the Rumsey-Sycamore Bed Spring Factory. In 1900, when he was fifteen, the boss put up a sign that said, "If this county goes for William Jennings Bryan [the more liberal candidate for President], there will be no work for two weeks." They voted for Bryan and were locked out for two weeks.

In their youth, all seven siblings worked as wandering actors in a troupe that offered plays—*The Trials of the Working Girl, Ingomar, the Barbarian, The Hunchback of Notre Dame*—around small-town Missouri. This was about 1910. However, they advanced to the professions because in those days credentialing was absent, and you could actually better yourself without an irrelevant college degree.

My father and two of his brothers became especially well-educated because, despite lack of formal education, they loved to read. My Uncle Ed read at night on a naval ship in World War I. Family legend has it that he used a torch, or flashlight. These were available by 1911 but it is possible he used a ship's lantern. As a result of his reading, he was one of six enlisted men who passed an exam to qualify for officer's training. Later he left the navy to become one of the most distinguished real estate entrepreneurs in Washington, D.C. He handled the famous Watergate Apartments where the break-in occurred that eventually led to the downfall of President Richard Nixon. He was the only one of the boys who did not have an alcohol problem, a disease prominent among Irish-American males (read Eugene O'Neill's *Long Day's Journey Into Night*). Uncle Henry was a distinguished journalist whose life and career were ruined by alcoholism. Uncle Jack became a naval commander who drank himself to death on Guam. I do not know whether Uncle Paul liked to read, although he did work at the Library of Congress.

My own generation, with one exception, has been largely exempt, so alcoholism is not in our genes. (Maybe reading is.) I suspect that since we were all college graduates the struggle to reach our potential was less grim. Perhaps it was just our professions because in the past the military and journalism were staffed by hard-drinking men (there were no women). Journalism was on the fringe of social respectability. The police were corrupt and did not like reporters saying so, which meant there were risks. My father's teeth on one side of his lower jaw were damaged when a policeman hit him with a blackjack.

My father was a drunk but not an alcoholic. He got drunk most evenings but was always sober the next day for work and was never jailed for public drunkenness. He often went to the police station to bail out his brothers. He was an excellent journalist but was out of work for about six years during the Great Depression of the 1930s. Like so many others, he was rescued by the onset of World War II, when he entered public service as a press-relations expert. Of all the family, he loved reading the most. He became highly educated, with a vocabulary larger than my own. To show off, he would do *The New York Times'* crossword puzzle in ink, just to advertise that he never made mistakes. He loved reading aloud, and when I was four read me all the novels of Charles Dickens. So I was born to reading. It simply never occurred to me not to read for pleasure.

TEENAGERS AND UNIVERSITIES

I have been a university lecturer for fifty-four years, and have taught at the University of Otago for the last forty-four. I have enjoyed my teaching more than I can say. But one thing has troubled me greatly. At universities in both America and New Zealand, universities such as Wisconsin State, Maryland, Cornell, Canterbury and Otago, I have noticed a trend: fewer and fewer students read great works of literature.

This is true even of my brightest students. It was true at Cornell, a university so élite that everyone was a bright student. Ask students what novelist they like the best and you get a blank, or some reference to the author of airport trash. And it is not just students: many of the university professors who are my colleagues no longer read outside the professional literature. Thus, if you read great books, as my Uncle Ed did by torchlight, you will know more than many university professors.

What has happened to young people from my time to this time? In 2008 and 2009 I was at the Russell Sage Foundation in New York City and studied test trends on vocabulary in America. The tests did not include specialized vocabulary, but sampled the vocabulary used in everyday life. Between 1948 and 2006, adults had made huge gains but schoolchildren, including those in their teens, had made very marginal gains. If we assume that the two age groups were similar in 1948, teenagers have fallen far behind: today fewer than nineteen percent of them have a non-specialized vocabulary that overlaps with that of the top fifty percent of their parents. I refer to their active vocabulary, the words they can use when they initiate a conversation. Passive vocabulary refers to the words you can understand when someone else uses them. Here the gulf between teenager and adult has grown very little, if at all.

In sum, in 1948 teenagers could both understand and use the vocabularies of their parents. In 2006 they could understand their parents but, to a surprising degree, could not initiate a conversation using adult language.

The damage is not permanent: they make up some of the gap if they go to university, and a few years after they have entered the world of work they make up the rest.

I have spoken of teenagers. As late as 1950, the term "teenager" did not exist. Those aged thirteen to nineteen wanted to become adults and enjoy the privileges of adults, such as lack of supervision and an income of their own. I never had money in my pocket except that given me by my parents for a specific purpose, say to do an errand or see a film. Today there is something called teenage subculture, and its members have the prerogatives of adulthood without the responsibilities. They have enormous purchasing power and, thanks to the automobile, a privacy that relieves them of close supervision. This subculture is so attractive that some young adults want to remain in it through their twenties and even their thirties, as parents who wish their aging children would get a job and move away from home are well aware.

Teenage subculture has developed its own English dialect. However, I had never realized that it had become so insulated that its members were not being socialized into their society's speech community.

It is an audio culture with a constant surround of popular music. It is a visual culture with leisure spent on the web and watching TV and films. Computer games are mesmerizing. Recently a sixteen-year-old killed his eighteen-year-old brother over access to PlayStation. No teenager in recent years has killed another in an argument over who was to get to read Tolstoy's *War and Peace*. Their subculture does not put a high priority on reading literature that requires concentration and wide general knowledge. After all, you are unlikely to enjoy *War and Peace* if the vocabulary is unfamiliar and you do not know who Napoléon was or where Russia is. The book runs to five volumes and 640 pages. If you love reading, you like long books because you never want a good book to end. If you read only as a last resort, when you cannot use electronic devices on an airplane, you will prefer to read a magazine about Paris Hilton.

I suggest that teenage culture not only gives young people a vocabulary gap, but also creates a love-of-reading deficit. While the former is closed with age, all too often the latter persists throughout life. Going to university does not do much good. Each university department assigns specialized reading within its field, and the more reading assigned the less time students have for leisure reading. If neither teenage nor university subcultures inculcate a love of reading, conveyancing in a law office is not going to step into the breach.

THE MAGIC REALM

This book will take you into a world far more wonderful than the world of work and entertainment. At university I try to make converts by assigning works of literature that shed light on human psychology, history or philosophy.

Some students respond by asking me to give them lists of books. Well, here is your list. But I also want to make converts of those who have not yet gone or will never go to university.

The educational establishment may ignore you but I will not. I remember my own family and how they educated themselves. Many in my running club have never been to university. Some of them are among the most intelligent and intellectually curious people I know. Some of them are better informed than university students about almost everything, except the narrow knowledge a graduate gets from majoring in physics or commerce or engineering. Some of my running companions know who Hitler was. As for my students, I once set an exam question about tyranny in the twentieth century. Only a few students could volunteer Hitler's name. The history of Germany from 1918 to 1945 is the story of how this man helped change what was perhaps the most civilized nation in Europe into an engine of cruelty almost beyond comprehension. Fortunately, a great novelist has charted the period for you: Erich Maria Remarque.

Let me convince you that you can make time to read. Read for forty minutes before bed each night to clear your mind of the day's concerns. Start with five great novels: Isaac Bashevis Singer, *The Slave*; Thornton Wilder, *The Bridge of San Luis Rey*; F. Scott Fitzgerald, *The Great Gatsby*; Erich Maria Remarque, *Spark of Life*; and Calder Willingham, *End as a Man*. I will make a bet: at least two of these will move you to tears and awaken emotions beyond anything pop culture can do.

LEARNING TO BE FREE

In a book in press, I try to give people the concepts they need to comprehend the complexities of the modern world. I want them to be free. I want them to be able to understand the world, rather than just be swept along by the river of time with no real comprehension of what is happening to them. But I stress that a full toolkit of concepts is not enough. You need to know something about science, and nations other than your own and their histories, and the human condition.

I am going to try to convince you that learning about the world can be delightful, because it can be done by reading for pleasure: novels, histories so well-written that they read like novels, poetry, and plays. In addition, there are some films you should try to see. I have chosen books not only for artistic merit but also for their power to educate. This means I have excluded some of the greatest novels ever written: their content would not acquaint you with a particular time or place. And I have included some books that are merely entertaining (only a few) because they are informative. The numbered works, those that will at least entertain, come to 200. Does that sound like a lot? Don't think of it that way. Education is a lifelong quest. Select out the ones you think you would enjoy, read them one by one, and luxuriate in the pleasure. The lot would take you only about five years if you read an hour or so a night.

They will help you to liberate yourself. You can know enough accounting to help a corporation evade their taxes, own a large house and drive an expensive car, and yet be no freer than a medieval serf, buffeted about by social forces he could not comprehend. Or you can enter a magic realm in which people are more interesting, informed, amusing and intelligent than anyone you encounter in everyday life. You can learn about our past, its wars and triumphs, you can learn about our time, its sins and joys, about America, Britain, the Russian soul, and why we will all have to settle for less if our planet is to survive.

SCIENCE AND EARLY CIVILIZATION

I will recommend some books that are not about mainstream science but are too good to miss. One of these is C.L. Barber, *The Story of Language* (1). Barber's views on the origins of language are interesting, but the main theme is how one small cluster of closely interrelated dialects—called Proto-Indo-European—that were spoken some seven thousand years ago in the vicinity of the Caspian Sea is the ancestor of most of the major languages of Europe, Iran and India, languages that are today the native tongues of approximately three billion people. In the process of discussing how these languages originated, Barber will introduce you to the prehistory of Europe.

The ancient Greeks invented the mathematics and science that led to Newton and Einstein: see the relevant chapters of Hugh Lloyd-Jones, *The Greek World* (2). They will awaken in you an admiration of Archimedes as a genius perhaps unsurpassed in our civilization: "so great a mathematician it seems impertinent to praise him." He solved geometrical problems that involve leaps of the imagination so breathtaking that he may have had at his disposal mathematical techniques not "discovered" until the seventeenth century. I suspect that you will not be able to resist reading the whole book and will thus learn about classical Greece in general.

A wonderful book in its own right and a window on pre-classical Greece is John Chadwick's *The Decipherment of Linear B* (3). It tells the tragic story of Michael Ventris, who died in a car crash in 1956 at the age of thirty-four. Before his death, he translated—with Chadwick's help— tablets from Knossos, an ancient city on the island of Crete. Ventris had a remarkable gift for languages; he spoke six European languages and read Latin and classical Greek. The brilliant deductions that led him to discover that Linear B was in fact pre-Homeric Greek read like a detective story. He established that the great civilization of ancient Crete was part of the mainland Mycenaean Greek civilization that preceded the dark ages of Greece and Homer.

To get the full story of how mathematics evolved from its earliest beginnings to the discovery of calculus by Newton and Leibnitz, read Alfred Hooper, *Makers of Mathematics* (4). Appropriately, there is a picture of an abacus on the cover. It is thought some such computational device led the Arabs to the crucial concept of zero as a number, rather than as the absence of anything.

This book will make you appreciate how much the progress of mathematics has depended on the development of mathematical notation. Originally problems were stated in prose. Imagine you had to solve a problem such as this: There is a number such that if the whole of it is added to one-seventh of it, the result will be nineteen. The Egyptian solution to this problem consists of a complex series of steps developed in a long essay leading to the conclusion that, if 16 and 17 were separated by eight "leaps", then the number would be at the fifth leap between them. We would simply write: $x + x/7 = 19$. Then the solution is easy. Take both sides of the equation times 7. This gives $7x + 1x = 7 \times 19$ (or 133). Thus $8x = 133$, which means $x = 16\,5/8$.

Cosmology has to do with the origins, history and dynamics of the physical universe, blending together what we know from astronomy to subatomic particles. Its development from the ancient Babylonians through Newton is wonderfully told in Arthur Koestler's *The Sleepwalkers* (5). The sections on Galileo and Kepler are particularly good. You will come away with some sympathy with Cardinal Bellarmine's treatment of Galileo. Thanks to Galileo's assumption that the planets moved in circles rather than ellipses, putting the sun at the center of the solar system led to absurdities such as the Earth going around an empty point in space near the sun. The book's first page offers a sample of Koestler's prose:

> *We can add to our knowledge, but we cannot sub-tract from it. When I try to see the universe as a Babylonian saw it around 300 BC, I must grope my way back to my own childhood. At the age of about four … I remember an occasion when my father pointed his finger at the white ceiling, which was decorated with a frieze of dancing figures, and explained that God was up there, watching me. I immediately became*

convinced that the dancers were God and henceforth addressed my prayers to them, asking them for protection against the terrors of day and night. Much in the same manner, I like to imagine, did the luminous figures on the dark ceiling of the world appear as living divinities to Babylonians and Egyptians. The Twins, the Bear, the Serpent were as familiar to them as my fluted dancers to me; they were thought to be not very far away, and they held power of life and death, harvest and rain.

Having reached Newton, you may want to read the excellent biography by Richard Westfall, *The Life of Isaac Newton* (6). Newton himself was less concerned with physics and mathematics than with the perversion of monotheism perpetuated by orthodox Christianity—the doctrine of the Trinity. Lisa Jardine in *The Curious Life of Robert Hooke* (7) will expose you to a genius who anticipated the concepts of Newton's new physics but simply did not have the mathematics to capitalize on his intuitions.

All was not theory. In *The Lunar Men: The Friends Who Made the Future* (8), Jenny Uglow portrays the men who formed the Lunar Society of Birmingham—toymaker Matthew Boulton, potter Josiah Wedgwood, James Watt, Joseph Priestley, Erasmus Darwin and others—who invented the kind of things that kick-started the Industrial Revolution. A few of their inventions, such as Erasmus Darwin's mechanical talking mouth, were not productive.

Post-Newtonian mathematics is for specialists, but there are many good books about post-Newtonian cosmology. My favorite is John Gribbin, *In Search of the Big Bang* (9). Gribbin tells the story of how two theories, Einstein's general theory of relativity (about the universe writ large) and quantum physics (about the minute world within the atom) came together to tell us that the universe began as a "big bang", when something infinitesimally small exploded to expand rapidly. At that time, gravity, the electromagnetic force, the nuclear force and the weak force were as yet undifferentiated, and if we can unlock the dynamics of the big bang we will have equations that unite all the forces of nature.

Gribbin writes of perhaps the most exciting moment of the twentieth century, when scientists realized that the radiation being picked up by Bell Laboratory's radio telescope was something that had originated near the beginning of the universe. The big bang universe was incredibly hot, but about 13.7 billion years ago, only 380,000 years after its inception, it cooled to the point that radiation decoupled from matter. The radiation unleashed is now very cool, thanks to the huge expansion of the universe. But it is a direct snapshot of the universe as it was billions of years before it had evolved creatures capable of picturing it.

In *The Universe: A Biography* (10), Gribbin updates his earlier work and paints a broad canvas from the origin of the universe to the origin of life to beyond the end of the universe. He has also written good biographies of Newton and Einstein. Another book, David Bodanis's, $E = mc^2$: A Biography of the World's Most Famous Equation (11), does a good job of explaining one of Einstein's three great discoveries and the role played by his predecessors, Maxwell, Faraday and Lavoisier.

Another dominant scientific theory is, of course, the theory of evolution. The most readable account of Darwin's life is Charles Darwin (12) by Adrian Desmond, James Moore and Janet Browne. It shows that the theory of evolution was not the diabolical concoction of a wicked man, but something forced on a good man by facts and logic. The description of the political, social and religious life of the time is excellent, although I am not entirely convinced that they influenced Darwin as directly as argued.

The best account of the current theory is Richard Dawkins' The Blind Watchmaker (13). The eighteenth-century theologian William Paley said that if he found a watch on the heath he would instantly postulate the existence of a watchmaker. Dawkins shows that complex organs such as eyes and wings need not have popped into existence as they are today. They evolved from humble beginnings (like a light-sensitive spot) through small mutations over long periods of time, with each mutation leaving the organ better adapted to promote survival than before. He explains why eagles can see better than humans do, why bats hear better, and why sharks have a better sense of smell.

Two books about evolution ought to be read as object lessons as to how great biologists who are philosophically naïve try to use it as a basis for ethics: George Gaylord Simpson's *The Meaning of Evolution* (14) and *Evolution in Action* (15) by Julian Huxley, Aldous Huxley's brother. Try to pick the flaw in their arguments. The key is that merely because something is a trend in evolution does not make it a good guide for human conduct. Just because the planets have (almost) circular orbits does not mean people should run around in circles.

You will find social science books under other headings, but as for social evolution, read Christopher Hallpike, *How We Got Here: From Bows and Arrows to the Space Age* (16). Hallpike stresses the role of the evolution of the human mind (not brain) in human development over the last 10,000 years. His earlier work was one of the inspirations of my book *What is Intelligence?*, which tells the story of how our minds have altered over just the last hundred years.

A book by Jared Diamond appeared in two editions. The original title was *The Rise and Fall of the Third Chimpanzee: How Our Animal Heritage Affects the Way We Live* (17). A later title is *The Third Chimpanzee: The Evolution and Future of the Human Animal*. Diamond explains why one species came to dominate its closest relatives, the chimpanzees, and why one group of humans, Eurasians, came to dominate the world. He discusses how the first contact between unequal civilizations almost always results in genocide (and yet we keep sending out space probes alerting advanced civilizations to our existence and location), and why technology may cause environmental degradation leading to extinction.

Diamond wrote another book, *Collapse: How Societies Choose to Fail or Succeed* (18). He searched history for societies faced with the possibility of environmental extinction, and analyzed both those that could not adapt and those that did. (There are a few success stories.) He will convince you that we are faced with an environmental crisis, even if you are a skeptic (as I am not) about global warming.

AMERICAN HISTORY

Just as Britain was the dominant power before 1914, America has been the dominant power since 1945. For fun—I am not sure it will really teach you much about America—read Calder Willingham's *The Gates of Hell* (19), a book of short stories and non-fiction that transcends the author's Southern origins. Today Willingham is largely forgotten, but he had a biting wit that showed through in screenplays ranging from *Paths of Glory* to *The Graduate*. He is irreverent in ways that offended sensibilities at the time (he presents openly gay characters) and will still offend some today (he sends up love manuals about women being divine instruments like violins).

A close second is Terry Southern, *The Magic Christian* (20). My favorite story is the altered version of *The Best Years Of Our Lives*, a cloying film about a man who comes back from World War II with metal hands. In the doctored version, there is a tender scene in which you see his mechanical hands groping beneath his fiancée's skirt.

Also for pure enjoyment, read *The Secret History* (21) by Donna Tartt. The students (who end up murdering one of their number) are too special to be representative of American undergraduates, but the writing is great. If you want a graphic portrait of contemporary American college life, go to Tom Wolfe, *I Am Charlotte Simmons* (22). However, the greatest novel in this genre is Calder Willingham, *End as a Man* (23). The boys are so real they practically pop out of the pages.

To learn American political history, read Gore Vidal's series of novels *Burr, 1876, Lincoln, Empire, Hollywood,* and *The Golden Age. Lincoln* (24) gives the best short account of the Civil War ever written. The extent of sympathy in Washington, D.C. for the South is nicely portrayed, and makes it clear that the only odd thing about the assassination of Abraham Lincoln is that it did not occur earlier. Read the histories of Bruce Catton for detail. All of the trilogy *Mr. Lincoln's Army, Glory Road* and *A Stillness at Appomattox* (25) are good, but the last is wonderful. The description of the deflation felt by black troops when it was decided their lives were "too precious" to risk is very affecting. Catton's *The Centennial History of the Civil War* (26) fills in the social, economic and political context of the war.

To understand the social and economic history of America you need to know what it has been like to be poor and working-class in America. The life of girls employed in the textile industry in the early nineteenth century is the theme of Samuel Hopkins Adams' *Sunrise to Sunset* (27). The title was the slogan of the bosses who said God had set the length of the working day, although this did not prevent them from bringing lamps into the factories when sunset came too soon for their taste. The girls tended to die young from the impurities in the air, but there were plenty more where they came from and they were cheaper to feed than men.

In his portrait of perhaps the greatest American who ever lived, *The Bending Cross: A Biography of Eugene Victor Debs* (28), Ray Ginger tells of the unequal struggle between labor and capital at the turn of the century—with troops mowing down strikers. It is little wonder that the IWW (Industrial Workers of the World) hijacked a train and drove it through the capital of Colorado in an attempt to assassinate the governor. (They got his chauffeur instead.)

The IWW published the *Little Red Songbook*. Get a copy if you can because it has some wonderful songs: "I Dreamed I Saw Joe Hill Last Night" ("The copper bosses killed you Joe, They shot you, Joe," says I. . . . And smiling with his eyes, Joe says, "What they forgot to kill went on to organize"); "The Preacher and the Slave"; "Might was Right" ("Might was right when Christ was hanged"); "Portland Revolution" ("And not a thing is moving, only Mayor Baker's bowels"). There are tributes to martyrs: murdered by the lumber trust; killed by a sheriff's posse on the free speech ship *Verona*. And to Frank Little, half Indian, half white man, all IWW. The back cover advertises sheet music handsomely done in appropriate colors. I have always wondered what the appropriate colors were for the combination "Child Laborers' Spring Song" and "Ancient Jewish Lullaby".

E.L. Doctorow is a great novelist. In *Ragtime* (29), he uses a middle-class family who live in New Rochelle, New

York to weave a panorama of what mattered in and to America from 1902 to 1914. Many characters are historical figures, including Harry Houdini, J.P. Morgan, Henry Ford, the anarchist Emma Goldman, Booker T. Washington, the Mexican revolutionary Emiliano Zapata, Sigmund Freud, Carl Jung, and Archduke Franz Ferdinand, whose assassination began World War I. It sounds awful but it is done wonderfully well. There is a black man named Coalhouse Walker whose crusade for justice attains success the moment before, probably at his own invitation, the police shoot him. Exhausted, he has no will left to live or fight. For the heyday of organized crime in America, see Doctorow's *Billy Bathgate* (30). Billy's Depression life is interrupted when he becomes a minor player in the gang of mobster Dutch Schultz.

The major work of John Dos Passos is the *U.S.A.* trilogy (31), comprising the novels *The 42nd Parallel*, *1919*, and *The Big Money*. The trilogy tells the stories of twelve fictional characters, and adds short biographies of people such as Woodrow Wilson and Henry Ford, to cover the evolution of American society during the first three decades of the twentieth century. Read about the terrible Dust Bowl, the great drought that hit the southwest in the 1920s, in John Steinbeck's, *The Grapes of Wrath* (32). The film with Henry Fonda is well worth seeing too. Jane Darwell gives an unforgettable performance as Ma Joad, the mother of the displaced family going to California. She had other great roles but once was reduced to playing a supporting role to Fabian in *Hound Dog Man*. Such is Hollywood. Do not neglect Steinbeck's short novels such as *Cannery Row* and *Tortilla Flat*.

In Saul Bellow, *The Adventures of Augie March* (33), you get the flavor of the Great Depression of the 1930s. The opening sentences foreshadow both the book's strong characters and its style, the latter marred by pretension and the irritating need of the author to show how well-educated he is: "I am an American, Chicago born—Chicago, that somber city—and go at things as I have taught myself, free-style. ... But a man's character is his fate, says Heraclitus, and in the end there isn't any way to disguise the nature of the knocks by acoustical work on the door or gloving the knuckles." To bring the fate of unskilled workers in America up to date, read the section in Tom Wolfe, *A Man in Full* (34) about the character who works in a suicidal freezing unit.

Americans fighting in World War II are sent up in the great comic novel *Catch-22* (35) by Joseph Heller. The scene in which a military court tries a soldier who has dared to criticize an officer is excellent. While on parade, the soldier turns to his left rather than to his right and brushes the sleeve of the man next to him. He is charged with felonious assault, attempted murder, and liking classical music. The colonel presiding over the court rises up "like a gigantic belch" and says he wants to tear the defendant's "stinking, cowardly body limb from limb".

(The colonel has not yet heard the charge.) The court recorder Popinjay irritates the colonel and is sent to the Solomon Islands to bury corpses. Heller's other novels needed editing, but he has a nice touch in *Good as Gold*. Gold is a Jew who believes Henry Kissinger was far too wicked to really be a Jew; he treasures newspaper reports such as one about Kissinger eating a ham sandwich.

A serious novel about the war is the one good novel by Norman Mailer, *The Naked and the Dead* (36). Mailer's later works developed his thoughts about the need for women to think they may die in childbirth to enjoy sex, and the "fact" that you catch cancer through cowardice. He wrote a wonderful account of the Emile Griffith versus Benny "Kid" Paret prizefight, which ended in death. That was the sort of thing he found congenial. He ruined his campaign for mayor of New York by stabbing his wife with an ice pick.

However, I must not be too holier than thou. When I belonged to the US Socialist Party, we ran a charismatic local black for mayor. A comrade met him during a fight in a bar. He was not difficult to recruit. At that time, when black children in New Haven were shown a teddy bear, forty percent of them identified it as a giant rat. Some children used to have their noses or lips bitten off by rats. White children living in poor black neighborhoods were not immune: my wife's elder sister used to terrify her by wiggling her foot under the covers of their bed and saying it was a rat.

The candidate irritated his wife by pawning things to finance his campaign, and when he went home to get his pistol to pawn she shot him. When taken to the hospital, he and others concocted a false story to protect her and the police tossed them all in jail. The party to raise funds for their defense was noisy. A policeman came to investigate, and the black guy who opened the door knocked him out and threw him into a closet without telling anyone. Other police came and found him. By now, the entire local committee of the Socialist Party was in jail. This took some of the bloom off our "good government" campaign.

In Philip Milton Roth, America found its voice about life from World War II to the present. The hysteria of the Cold War anti-communist witch-hunt is caught in *I Married a Communist* (37): "Mommy, there are men in our house who are speaking *Russian*." The first volume of the second Zuckerman trilogy, *American Pastoral* (38), tells of a virtuous man, Seymour "Swede" Levov, and the purgatory he endures after his daughter becomes a terrorist during the late 1960s, and then a Janist starving herself to death because it is wrong to kill and eat living things.

All of Roth's novels are good. *The Anatomy Lesson* has a minor character who makes pornographic films, but has principles: "There are some things I won't do, like showing women having sex with dogs. A dog is never the same after that—it scrambles their brains completely." *Operation Shylock: A Confession* will convince you that not all Jewish-Americans are Israeli chauvinists.

There is a host of regional literature. About the early south-west United States, Willa Cather's *Death Comes for the Archbishop* (39) is gripping, and has some striking characters, such as the priest who enslaves the native population, only to be executed by them after he accidentally kills one of his servants. His dinner guests see what is coming and hastily abandon him. About the small-town Midwest, read Sherwood Anderson *Winesburg, Ohio* (40). The book is much resented in Ohio but eventually Anderson was punished: he choked to death on an olive in a martini. (The olive had a toothpick in it.)

William Faulkner's novels are set in Mississippi. His style is too convoluted for my taste but he introduces a wide array of characters: slaves, their descendants, poor whites, and southern aristocrats. His most readable novel is *The Sound and the Fury* (41), perhaps because most of it is told through the mouths of ordinary people (if any of his characters can be considered ordinary): Dilsey, who is a black servant, and three brothers, one of whom describes the period leading up to his suicide, and another of whom is mentally handicapped (and whose style suffers thereby).

After he received the Nobel Prize, Faulkner gave money to help black students attend Rust College in Holly Springs, Mississippi. The money might have been better spent out of state. Since 1866, Rust College has had few distinguished alumni. There was a Methodist bishop (class of 1902), a really good operatic soprano (circa 1920), and a pop singer (circa 1977). Ida Bell Wells attended the college but did not actually graduate: the president expelled her for having a rebellious spirit. He was correct. She refused to give up her seat on a train in 1884, thus anticipating the black woman who, almost seventy years later, refused to give up her seat on a bus and launched Martin Luther King. Wells was also a distinguished journalist, a civil rights militant, and a leader in the campaign against lynching.

Erskine Caldwell's *Tobacco Road* (42) is set in Augusta, Georgia during the Great Depression. Do not see the 1941 film, which is just a vulgar comedy. Jeeter Lester is a poor white tenant farmer whose family is reduced to starvation, but who will not abandon his farm for work in the mill, where wages keep a person just above starvation. Two of the characters are deformed: one of them has a nose like that of a pig. Their main concern is that they be buried properly. For example, Jeeter is afraid that his body will be left in the storage shed, where it might be eaten by rats—his father's face had been half-eaten by rats before his body was found. Perhaps there is something in Nietzsche's dictum that depravity and misery are productive of great art.

The best book on the politics of the South in the 1930s is Robert Penn Warren, *All the King's Men* (43). It is a fictionalised account of Senator Huey Long of Louisiana, who died at the height of his power in 1935, killed either by an assassin or by his bodyguards shooting at what they thought was an assassin. Long had a program ("Share the wealth") to help the poor that was far more ambitious and egalitarian than the "New Deal" of President Franklin D. Roosevelt. He is painted as an idealist who was forced to use every trick of corruption and patronage to advance his program. (He was a quick learner.) His possible assassin was an aristocratic idealist who could not compromise. The last straw was when he learned of Long's affair with his sister and felt personally dishonored. The narrator is a cynical student of history—until the end, when he perceives that the source of his cynicism is a disdain for his parents based on ignorance. All of the characters are wonderful and the portrayal of the South of the day photographic.

For a great play about the South in transition toward what it is today (somewhat less depraved), see *A Streetcar Named Desire* (44) by Tennessee Williams. The film with Vivien Leigh as Blanche and Marlon Brando as Stanley Kowalski is very good. Blanche is old South, but the ancestral home is gone and she goes to stay with her sister Stella, who is married to Kowalski. He is a Polish immigrant and foreshadows the new South. Blanche and Kowalski do not get on and Blanche eventually goes to an asylum. There really is a streetcar in New Orleans named *Desire* after its destination, Desire Street.

Tom Wolfe's novels have already been mentioned but I want to add that two take us to the South of today. *A Man in Full* shows the white élite of Atlanta, Georgia in all of its nastiness, as well as the exuberance of the new black middle class. *I am Charlotte Simmons* illustrates the end of the isolation of the rural South.

The western or "cowboy" novel is considered low-brow, but two authors showed what could be done with frontier settings. E.L. Doctorow's first novel *Welcome to Hard Times* (45) describes what life was really like: grim, and no points for being a hero—they die young. The only real accomplishment is survival, and a brothel can be the growth industry that makes a town economically viable. The Robert Altman film *McCabe & Mrs Miller* is recommended to complete the picture.

If you like the paintings of Andrew Wyeth or Grahame Sydney, you will like the spare style of Dorothy Johnson. *The Man Who Shot Liberty Valance* (46) contains four stories. The title story is good, but not as good as the other three. *A Man Called Horse* is about a British aristocrat captured by some American Indians. He is enslaved and literally treated as a horse. He wins a place in society and finds himself by helping a woman who desperately needs him if she is to survive under tribal custom. *Hanging Tree* charts the interaction between a man who falls in love with a helpless would-be schoolteacher and the schoolteacher's naïveté: she squanders the help he gives her without her knowledge. *Lost Sister* describes the dissonance between a family and a sister who is reclaimed from the tribe that reared her, and who has no sense of self outside it.

AMERICA BROODS

One of the things that made America introspective from its earliest days was the diversity of its population, not just its black and Hispanic minorities but also its abundant white minorities. Each of these groups had its own version of American history, colored by its unique experience. This kind of brooding about what America was, and what it was becoming as immigrants flocked to its shores, may explain why the United States is intoxicated with self-criticism.

When Oscar Handlin wrote *The Uprooted* (47) about American immigrants, he suddenly realized that their history was the history of America. If you want to know why Americans are so religious and conservative (the two often go together), reflect on the fact that many came from rural poverty into alien cities, found themselves losing their language and identity, and the only familiar institution they could carry with them was their church. They also wanted to get rich and to believe it was possible to get rich, and this did not make socialism attractive.

As an Irish-American married to a Jewish-American, I have a special interest in two groups. Start with the famine in Ireland (An Gorta Mór in Gaelic) by reading Cecil Woodham-Smith's *The Great Hunger: Ireland 1845–1849* (48). Over a decade, out of a population of eight million a million died and a million emigrated; even today the island's total population is still just over six million. If you want to know why the Irish came to hate the English Crown, in 1845 Ottoman Sultan Abdülmecid I declared his intention of sending 10,000 pounds sterling to famine-wracked Ireland; Queen Victoria asked him to send only 1000 because she had sent only 2000. The Sultan sent the lesser amount but secretly dispatched three ships full of food. English courts tried to block the ships. However, Ottoman sailors smuggled the food ashore in Drogheda Harbour. The Crown did not try to intercept the $710 sent by American Choctaw Indians.

The first Australian I ever met was an Irish taxi driver in Sydney. He was a true Irishman. As soon as he heard the name Flynn, he began, to my alarm, to look back over his shoulder and tell me about his country. Sir Robert Menzies, the prime minister, had bought a knighthood from the Queen by sinking millions into an opera house financed by the working man. Some similar conspiracy was the cause of the rising price of vegetables. Wherever the English had gone they had, he said, "rooted" the people. Since I was going on to Tasmania, he warned me I would encounter many albinos "because they are so inbred".

I should add that the Irish blamed the English Crown, not the English people, for their woes, and that today they have put their past behind them. They do, however, have to be tolerant of English jokes about Irish stupidity. I have never had the heart to tell my hosts what Irish jokes about the English are like. They are unprintable. But as a hint, they focus on the sexual proclivities and performance of the upper classes. The males are supposed to have a fondness for bestiality, and the females all the liveliness of a corpse.

As for Irish in America, *How the Irish Became White* (49) by Noel Ignatiev is rambling and flawed, but the information is there and the main theme valid. Up to about 1920, both in America and Britain, many of the Anglo-Saxon majority put Irish below blacks and portrayed them as animals, albeit higher animals (see the cartoons in *Punch*, which run to chimpanzees). My father often read "No Irish need apply, black man preferred" ads in the newspaper. Eventually, the Irish made it. A turning point was when Al Smith ran for president in 1928. He lost because he was an Irish Catholic ("vote against rum, Romanism and rebellion"), but he showed what was possible.

A Tree Grows in Brooklyn (50) by Betty Smith is a novel about an Irish-American family in New York between 1900 and 1920. I have never met anyone who did not love reading it. The father is handsome, charming and talented, and has three brothers who are similar. All of them drink themselves to death by the age of thirty-five. The father's family loves him despite the hardships his addiction entails. His wife struggles to give her three children a decent upbringing despite their constant poverty. Her favorite is her son, and her relationship with the narrator, her daughter

Francie, is strained, although both respect the quality of the other. The mother finally marries a local politician and Francie escapes to university.

James T. Farrell's novels portray the Irish experience in Chicago in the 1930s and the ambiguous role of the Catholic church, his best being *Studs Lonigan* (51). Mary McCarthy's *Memories of a Catholic Girlhood* (52) tells the story of a wealthy girl—ordinary Irish called them "lace curtain Irish". Eugene O'Neill's fifty-one plays range well beyond Irish America, but his masterpiece *Long Day's Journey into Night* (53) portrays the tragedy of many Irish-American families: the males are alcoholics (of course) and the mother on morphine (not common).

Irving Howe, *World of Our Fathers: The Journey of the East European Jews to America and the Life They Found and Made* (54) is so good it is almost sufficient. I have already mentioned Philip Roth's novels. To look into the world of highly orthodox Jews, read the novels of Chaim Potok. In *The Chosen* (55) he tells of a boy who wants to study psychology, but whose father is the leader of a Hasidic sect and assumes his son will succeed him as rabbi. There is a wonderful description of a game between orthodox and less orthodox baseball teams that amounts to a spiritual war. In *My Name is Asher Lev* (56), a gifted boy is part of a Hasidic Jewish family who see art as at best a waste of time and at worst as sacrilege. His masterpiece is a painting of the crucifixion, which so offends his parents and community that he is asked to leave.

In his books of journalistic essays, Tom Wolfe says much about American ethnic culture. In *Radical Chic & Mau-Mauing the Flak Catchers* (57), he sends up the attempt of the Jewish composer Leonard Bernstein to build bridges between himself and the Black Panthers at a social gathering at his apartment. Bernstein tried: he hired whites to replace his usual black butler and maid. Wolfe's account did something to bring the two parties together. The Black Panthers reacted: "You mean that dirty, blatant, lying, racist dog who wrote that fascist disgusting thing in *New York* magazine?"

The interplay of Anglo-Saxons with Irish with Jews with blacks in New York is a feature of Wolfe's *The Bonfire of the Vanities* (58). A Jewish cop's highest aspiration is to be mistaken for a "harp", a fearless Irish cop. The central character is a "master of the universe", a Wall Street player. Early on, he wants an excuse to go outside to get away from his wife so he can phone his mistress. The doorman of his apartment building looks on in wonder as he tries to drag his dog, whining, feet braced, claws dug into the carpet, out from under the building's awning into torrential rain. If you want to know what it is like to be the wife of a master of the universe, read Sue Kaufman, *Diary of a Mad Housewife* (59).

For the Irish-Italian ethnic mix peculiar to New Orleans, see John Kennedy Toole's funny book *A Confederacy of Dunces* (60). The fact that Toole published nothing during his lifetime contributed to his suicide in 1969. His book was published posthumously in 1980 and immediately won the Pulitzer Prize for Fiction.

Black America leads naturally to the literature on self-criticism, in that America can hardly discuss blacks without being self-critical. The best history of blacks after slavery up to the civil rights movement is C. Vann Woodward's *The Strange Career of Jim Crow* (61), published in 1955. There are many books about the lynching of blacks but try to get to hear "Strange Fruit", sung by Billie Holiday. Abel Meeropol, a Jewish high-school teacher, published the poem under the pen name Lewis Allan in 1936. Between 1882 and 1968, there were 3437 lynchings of blacks (and 1293 lynchings of whites). Meeropol and his wife later adopted Robert and Michael Rosenberg, the sons of Julius and Ethel Rosenberg who were convicted of espionage and executed by the United States. Also see *Killers of the Dream* (62) by Lillian Smith about what segregation did to the mind of the South.

About the early civil rights movement, go to the source, Martin Luther King Jr., *Stride Toward Freedom* (63). It all started when Rosa Parks refused to give up her seat on a bus to a white man and was arrested. Also read King's *Letter from the Birmingham Jail*: "In deep disappointment I have wept over the laxity of the church. There can be no deep disappointment where there is not deep love." Sunday morning was the most segregated time in America. Soon after King's letter, the Sixteenth Street Baptist Church in Birmingham was bombed, killing four little black girls.

They had heard a sermon entitled "The Love that Forgives" and been among twenty-six who later assembled to pray.

Since blacks have got legal equality, things have got a lot more complicated. For two contrasting (but not always contradictory) views, read Thomas Sowell, *Black Education: Myths and Tragedies* (64), and chapters two to four of my *Where Have All the Liberals Gone?*

Thorstein Veblen's *The Theory of the Leisure Class* (65) is the most searching critique of nineteenth-century America in the heyday of ostentatious wealth amidst poverty. Veblen points out that angels wear white robes to make it clear they do not belong to the blue-collar classes. He also has a penetrating wit: the dog is man's favorite pet because it is the animal most slavish in its disposition and nastiest in its habits.

Ruth Benedict in *Patterns of Culture* (66) used anthropology as a mirror to allow Americans to see themselves from the outside. She noted the Kwakiutl Indians, who do not seek love in marriage but an opportunity to target the father of the bride. At the marriage ceremony, if you can afford to destroy more possessions than he can, he is shamed and often commits suicide. The corporate rich who marry a trophy wife for display along with their other possessions (seven homes, private airplane) are not far behind them. Nor are average Americans who spend their life in debt so they can have bigger and bigger cars and houses. Arthur Miller's play *Death of a Salesman* (67) shows the toll taken by the make-money-or-die ethic of middle

America. Willy Loman atones for his life of failure by killing himself "accidentally" so his family will be endowed
with his life insurance.

For a machine-gun critique of World War II America,
read a book my circle all read in high school, namely
Philip Wylie's *Generation of Vipers* (68). The chapters on
"momism" and "the common man" hit home. Circa 1946,
Wylie added a note predicting that the proliferation of
nuclear weapons would eventually force America to introduce surveillance of a kind destructive of individual liberty.
Therefore, he advised knocking anyone flat who tried to
break America's nuclear monopoly (a policy also endorsed
by Bertrand Russell).

Kurt Vonnegut's novels cover World War II to the
present. His mission is to make complacency impossible—
that is, to force Americans to face up to every horrible and
ludicrous thing that goes on. The strangeness of American
politics is the theme of *God Bless You, Mr. Rosewater* (69)
(a blend of Roosevelt and Goldwater). Rosewater meets a
poet who hates money, but when endowed with some by
Rosewater he becomes obsessed with writing the kind of
poetry his patron would like. Rosewater tells him his
favorite poem: "We don't piss in your ashtrays, so don't
throw cigarette butts in our urinals."

The fascist right gets its turn in *Mother Night* (70). The
hero is an American spy who has infiltrated Hitler's prop-
aganda organization. When Hitler asks for some inspiring
funeral oratory, he sends him Lincoln's Gettysburg address.

Hitler is deeply moved by words capturing what any good Aryan feels when contemplating the fallen warrior, but he has a question. The author's name is Abraham—could he be Jewish?

After the war, the hero meets Robert, the Black Führer of Harlem, who is employed by the very white Reverend Doctor Jones. Each believes the other will have to be exterminated, but in the meantime they have much in common. Some dialogue:

> *"I tell this Reverend gentleman here the same thing every morning (when) I give him his hot cereal for breakfast. The colored people are gonna rise up in righteous wrath, and they're gonna take over the world. White folks gonna finally lose! The colored people gonna have hydrogen bombs all their own. They working on it right now. Pretty soon gonna be Japan's turn to drop one. The rest of the colored folks gonna give them the honor of dropping the first one."*
>
> *Where are they going to drop it?*
>
> *"China, most likely."*
>
> *On other colored people?*
>
> *He looked at me pityingly.*
>
> *"Who ever told you a Chinaman was a colored man?"*

In *Jailbird* (71), Vonnegut expresses in one sentence the flow of America's thinking about its role in the post World War II world: "Our armed forces were to be a thunderbolt with which we could vaporize any new, would-be Hitler, anywhere in the world. No sooner had the people of a country lost their freedom than the United States of America would arrive to give it back again." Particularly nice is the conglomerate that buys *The New York Times*, not because it wants the newspaper but because one of its subsidiaries is the second largest cat-food company in the world. Considering what *The New York Times* is like, who could question their priorities?

Nathanael West also wrote about the dark side of American life. His *Miss Lonelyhearts* (72) uses New York during the Great Depression as a symbol of evil. If you think you have read tragic novels about Hollywood, read *The Day of the Locust* (73).

THE HUMAN CONDITION I

Every now and then we will have an interlude to identify something that will keep cropping up in the literature of nation after nation. In America, Thornton Wilder put it as follows: "How terrifying and glorious the role of man if, indeed, without guidance and without consolation he must create from his own vitals the meaning of his existence and write the rules whereby he lives." This dilemma of modern man is universal but has a special application to Americans, at least those who realize that neither affluence nor some glorious group membership (being an American) provides a solution.

John Barth wrote two novels about this problem. In *The Sot-Weed Factor* (74) (sot-weed is tobacco) nothing is what it seems. Ebenezer comes to doubt even the existence of the major persons of the day and finds his judgment paralyzed by the absence of absolute standards. In *The End of the Road* (75), the main character is literally paralyzed by indecision—nothing seems better than anything else. Rebecca Goldstein's novel *The Mind-Body Problem* (76), about what she found at Princeton, aside from various lovers, shows the initial response of American academic philosophers. They were not interested in fundamental problems, but thought they could all be dissolved by analysis of "ordinary language" (of all things).

The greatest work of art on this theme, and what many consider the greatest American novel, is F. Scott Fitzgerald's *The Great Gatsby* (77). The only characters with ideals are Tom, obsessed with a crazy ideal (the need to keep down the colored races), and Gatsby, infected with a quixotic fantasy that he can abolish the past and reclaim his long-lost love as she was as a girl, unmarked by her marriage and adult life. Fitzgerald asks what America has been all about: no more than a scramble for money and status that blinds people to the fact they are empty of purpose?

Fitzgerald writes like a lyric poet. The spell America once cast: "As the moon rose higher the inessential houses began to melt away until gradually I became aware of the old island here that flowered once for Dutch sailors' eyes —a fresh, green breast of the new world. Its vanished trees, the trees that had made way for Gatsby's house, had once pandered in whispers to the last and greatest of all human dreams; for a transitory enchanted moment man must have held his breath in the presence of this continent, compelled into an aesthetic contemplation he neither understood nor desired, face to face for the last time in history with something commensurate to his capacity for wonder."

Fitzgerald wrote Gatsby in 1925. Contrast his troubled mind with the certitude of the poem Emily Dickinson wrote some fifty years earlier:

I never saw a moor,
I never saw the sea;
Yet know I how the heather looks,
And what a wave must be.

I never spoke with God,
Nor visited in heaven;
Yet certain am I of the spot
As if the chart were given.

And compare Dickinson's hymn on God and nature to the thoughts of a contemporary poet (Flynn, *O God Who Has a Russian Soul*):

The word speaks of wonder
But who speaks the word?
Nature teaches nothing
'Til the mind has heard.

Once we stood on high peaks
Faith full of intent
Now must we create selves
Worthy of ascent.

What climber boasts of flight
On an angel wing,
What son self crucify
To save Christ the King?

The odd thing about Fitzgerald and his generation is that they seem to have expected their time to hand them a set of ideals worthy of regard. Perhaps this was an attitude they inherited from a now vanished religious faith: God or the bible is supposed to tell you what to believe about good and evil. It never seems to occur to them that each person, as Thornton Wilder says, "must create from his own vitals the meaning of his existence and write the rules whereby he lives."

The jazz age of Fitzgerald, with its money, fast cars, endless parties and easy sex, held many temptations to become disillusioned or cynical. But what age does not pose a host of temptations to be self-obsessed—at worst a hedonist, at best a person lamenting that "something is missing". Today there are signs of an evolving moral maturity. From the slaughter the United States prolonged in Vietnam to the slaughter that has resulted from its incursions into the Middle East, there has emerged a public that demands their country justify its wars as somehow protecting mankind from the spread of nuclear weapons, or some other purpose above national interest. The policy élite no longer dares draft ordinary people to fight, but depends on a professional army. And it attempts to sell every war in moral terms: the country is overthrowing a tyrant, or preventing a madman from threatening the world with the bomb.

When I was a child, we were all assigned to read a short story, "The Man Without a Country", by Edward Everett

Hale. It ends with the following lunatic tirade: "For your country, boy, and for that flag, never dream a dream but of serving her as she bids you, though the service carry you through a thousand hells. No matter what happens to you, no matter who flatters you or abuses you, never look at another flag, never let a night pass but you pray God to bless that flag. Remember, boy, that behind all these men . . . behind officers and government, and people even, there is the Country Herself, your Country, and that you belong to her as you belong to your own mother. Stand by her, boy, as you would stand by your mother!" Few teachers in America would assign that story today.

LATIN AMERICA

For fun, start with Graham Greene, *Our Man in Havana* (78). An Englishman sketches gigantic vacuum cleaners to convince the British secret service there are weapons of mass destruction concealed in rural Cuba. (He wants to get on the payroll.) The chief of police is about as sympathetic a character as someone can be who heads an organization that tortures people. This was under the dictator Fulgencio Batista—whom the United States supported because he sold his country out to American corporate interests—until Castro overthrew him in 1959. Castro did much to alleviate the lot of the poor in terms of public health and literacy, but disgraced himself by refusing to hold elections. Better a benevolent than a purely self-interested dictator, but it was a pity.

There is a book that will disabuse you of any notion that the Spaniards subdued the peoples of Latin America because of genetic superiority. In *Guns, Germs, and Steel: The Fates of Human Societies* (79), Jared Diamond uses biogeography to explain the fact that Europeans had dense populations, large ocean-going ships, and iron tools and weapons. For example, Europe's indigenous plants and animals were much easier to domesticate. Spaniards rode to war on horses but Indians could not ride out to meet them on tapirs. That those of Spanish descent despise those of indigenous origin is the curse of Latin America to the present day, aside from the meddling in its affairs by the United States.

Latin America is too diverse to cover each nation. I will focus mainly on Mexico, Peru and Chile. Presumably, American readers will first want to know something about their neighbor to the south, whose immigrants to the United States are so much in the news.

MEXICO

To orient reading you may do about Mexico (and to give you my slant), here is a brief history. From 1876 to 1910, Porfirio Díaz was dictator, in defiance of the Mexican constitution. Mexico entered a period of industrialization, which created a working class to join a class of exploited peasants. In 1910 a revolution began, involving three groups. Modernizers wanted to build a centralized modern state, and did not want democracy to hamper their efforts or undermine their privileges. Organized workers wanted better conditions and democracy so they could have political influence. Landless peasants wanted decentralization and land reform. By 1920 the revolution had cost about two million lives.

The modernizers ultimately prevailed, partly because the workers and peasants were divided: the former thought the latter backward, superstitious and religious. Power and wealth was (and still is) concentrated among an élite of largely European descent. The vehicle of their dominance became the PRI, or Institutional Revolutionary Party, founded in 1929. Revolutionary violence diminished but did not really end until 1934, when Lárzaro Cárdenas became president. Cardenas tried to bring democracy and socialism to Mexico, but the PRI degenerated into a party of corruption and electoral fraud. It was "undefeated" until 2000, when, in a real election, Vicente Fox became president. In 2006 Felipe Calderón succeeded him.

Jack London's "The Mexican" (80) is a short story first published in *The Saturday Evening Post* in 1911. About a prizefight, it captures the spirit of the revolution. Also see the film *Viva Zapata!* The life and role of the revolutionary Emiliano Zapata are romanticized, but his struggle against General Victoriano Huerta (who betrayed the revolution) is well portrayed. John Steinbeck wrote the screenplay and the film stars Marlon Brando, Jean Peters and Anthony Quinn. Pancho Villa was one of Zapata's allies. He is remembered in America as a bank robber but Mexico reveres him. In passing, all of Jack London's boxing stories are worth reading: "The Abysmal Brute"; "The Game"; and "A Piece of Steak", a heart-rending account of the fate of an English working-class boxer.

Carlos Fuentes wrote several historical novels. I cannot recommend them as books you are sure to enjoy: they are spoiled by lapses into florid prose and boring literary conceits (more on this later). But if you have a special interest in Mexico, they are mostly readable. An American writer, Ambrose Bierce, went to Mexico in 1913 to accompany Pancho Villa's army, and a year later simply disappeared. *The Old Gringo* speculates on what might have happened, and fleshes out the image of Villa. *The Death of Artemio Cruz* is a series of flashbacks about a tycoon whose life story covers Mexican history from 1913 up to almost 1960. *The Years with Laura Díaz* is about a photographer and covers 1905 to 1972. The latter is the better of the two.

Oscar Lewis, *Children of Sanchez* (81) is an excellent study of a family living in a Mexico City slum in the 1950s. Jesus, the father, is a product of the past, and ironically is better adapted to the present than his adult children, Manuel, Roberto, Consuelo and Marta. The book is so good it was initially banned in Mexico.

Modernization is making Mexico more and more like the United States, but with a poverty level rather like that of the 1930s Depression, hence a flood of illegal immigrants across the border. I suspect that those who rail against this will be defeated by history, and something like the European Community will evolve, embracing Canada, the United States and Mexico. Fuentes' *A New Time for Mexico* (82) has a chapter on this well worth reading. He points out that much US business wants the immigrants as a pool of cheap labor to do jobs Americans will not do. He concedes that an economic community may mean more jobs "offshored" to Mexico. This is happening anyway: American corporations are sending their manufacturing and service work to India and the Philippines. Why not invest in Mexico? The more prosperous it becomes, the less an open border will be resented.

PERU

Mexico's politics became increasingly class-oriented as admixture reduced the Indian population to only 8.5 percent. In Peru, the ethnic breakdown is Indian forty-five percent, mestizo (mixed Spanish and Indian) forty percent, blacks five percent and Europeans ten percent. Until recently, the Indians were considered subhuman and enslaved or slaughtered. This was generally the case in Latin America. Try to see *The Mission* (83), a British film about a Jesuit missionary who, circa 1750, fights to protect the Guaraní Indians from enslavement. The musical score by Italian composer Ennio Morricone is worth hearing for itself. The Guaraní live in Paraguay and some liberties have been taken with history, but the film captures the racial attitudes of the time.

Thornton Wilder in *The Bridge of San Luis Rey* (84) gives a vibrant account of Spanish life in eighteenth-century Peru. The book transcends time and place because of its style and theme. The prose reads as if Wilder were under a spell cast upon him by the characters. He uses an "act of God"—a bridge snaps, casting those on it into the gulf below—to ask whether life has any meaning beyond that we give it. The last sentence: "There is a land of the living and a land of the dead and the bridge is love, the only survival, the only meaning." As for the Indians, as a bishop says, their lot is so terrible that it is "better to avert the mind." Do not be put off this book by the fact that Tony Blair likes to quote from it.

Peru has never come to terms with the fact that it is predominantly a non-white nation. Indians are still portrayed as backward and inferior, and perform the hardest and least remunerative forms of labor. Amazon Indian groups face cultural extinction as a result of oil exploration, agricultural production and mining colonizing campaigns. The Indians have become better organized and in 2009 actually won a test of strength, blockading rivers and roads to defend their territory against legislation that allowed foreign companies to exploit the Amazon forest. After 334 deaths and police failing to breach their lines, the legislation was repealed.

The Amazon Indian confederation is their most effective voice, but desperation has prompted some to enlist in revolutionary groups. Ann Patchett based her novel *Bel Canto* (85) on the Lima crisis of 1996. Fourteen members of the Túpac Amaru Revolutionary Movement (MRTA) took hostages at a party at the official residence of the Japanese ambassador. Patchett's portrayal of their leader makes their psychology powerfully clear: "why anyone would want a long life escaped him." The captors and captives develop relationships that humanize them and make you wish there were some alternative to a tragic outcome. For example, a hostage opera star discovers that a young terrorist is a wonderful natural talent and begins tutoring him.

Mario Vargas Llosa's novels have a contemporary setting, and reflect the life of Peru's urbanized middle class. In *Aunt Julia and the Scriptwriter* (86), the main character is an eighteen-year-old who works for a radio station and has an affair with his aunt. The station specializes in soap operas. It used to buy the scripts by the pound from Cuba but has hired a Bolivian scriptwriter. He writes exciting scripts. He gives both a priest and a Jehovah's Witness the same name, suggesting they are much the same. (Peru is a Catholic country in which Jehovah's Witnesses are unwelcome.) There are many demeaning references to Argentines. Two approach him about an episode in which he says that Argentine women enjoy eating the lice they pick out of their children's hair. He dismisses them abruptly: "Go sing tangos and wash your ears."

CHILE

Pablo Neruda of Chile is Latin America's greatest poet. He renders comprehensible how the sufferings of its people could drive a humane man into the arms of Stalinism. The best biography is *Pablo Neruda: A Passion for Life* (87) by Adam Feinstein. Unfortunately, Feinstein is too serious to include some details from Neruda's memoirs, such how he befriended an orangutan. The pair would walk hand in hand through the botanical gardens of Rangoon, and then have beer in the cafeteria. *Canto General* contains the poems in which Neruda says most about the people of Latin America, but I know of no good English translation. The poems translated by Mark Eisner in *The Essential Neruda: Selected Poems* (88) may be incentive enough to learn Spanish.

Chile's great trauma was in 1973, when the military overthrew the Marxist president Salvador Allende. Initially, Allende had achieved impressive economic growth while nationalizing banking and major industry, redistributing income from rich to poor, reducing unemployment, and introducing land reform. Unfortunately, he was foolish enough to turn Chile into a base for Soviet operations in Latin America. Whether his economic policies were sustainable is debatable, because the society began to unravel. The opposition, abetted by the United States, sabotaged the economy; the government made mistakes such as introducing price controls (which always produce shortages and a black market); and workers and peasants seized factories and estates that then became dysfunctional.

After the coup, General Augusto Pinochet instituted a reign of terror that lasted from 1973 to his defeat in an election held in 1989. Over 3000 people were murdered, tens of thousands were tortured, and 30,000 fled the country. In 2000, Chile elected a Democratic Socialist president, Richard Lagos, who introduced unemployment insurance, spread subsidized health care, and extended schooling to twelve years. Michelle Bachelet, another Socialist, became Chile's first woman president in 2006, but three years later a center-right candidate was elected.

Isabel Allende is a first cousin once removed of Salvador Allende. In 1982 her book *The House of the Spirits* (89) created a sensation. It was called both a work of genius and trash. It is neither but rather a good novel that would have been improved by editing. It follows three generations of women from a family headed by a patriarch whose life spans much of twentieth-century Chile. It shows how Allende's victory in 1970 was the inevitable result of a gradual rise in Socialist support. Prior to 1938 an élite manipulated elections to defeat the left, but center-left governments were in power from 1938 to 1958. The book also shows why the élite simply could not stomach Allende's victory.

Also read Isabel Allende's *My Invented Country* (90). As usual, the European settlers decimated the Indians, who now comprise only ten percent of the population. To "clear" the far south, hunters got a bounty for every pair of ears they cut from an Indian corpse.

The book is partisan and rather chatty but clarifies much that I had found confusing about Chilean society: why Pinochet promised an election that led to his defeat (he felt a need for legitimacy in a nation to whom legal forms are important); whether the election of a female president meant male domination was not too oppressive, at least in Latin American terms (men and most women still have stereotypes that favor sons over daughters, and turn a blind eye to male chauvinism); why the Catholic church is so strong (it has been consistently on the side of the poor); and why, despite Social Democratic presidents since 2000, there are such extremes of rich and poor. (Until 2006, when the left lost power, the senate was a curb because of its appointed members. Today, the rich plus a technocratic élite control the economy. Underlying all there is a rigid economic hierarchy based on race, with gradations by skin color from top to bottom.)

BOOKS TOO GOOD TO MISS

The novel by Gabriel García Márquez *Love in the Time of Cholera* (91) is set in Colombia and the action takes place between 1880 and 1930. It will convince you that what Anglo-Saxons call romantic love pales beside the passions of Latin Americans. The first volume of García Márquez's memoirs has been translated into English. In *Living to Tell the Tale*, he covers his life up to 1950. The descriptions of the artistic scene in Bogotá, the nation's capital, will convince you that New York and London are rather tame. Lurking in the background is Colombia's troubled history. García Márquez describes the Bananeras massacre, a strike in 1928 that escalated into the slaughter of United Fruit Company workers, and the 1948 uprising that destroyed much of Bogotá.

V.S. Naipaul is a master of English prose. His book *The Middle Passage* (92) analyzes the West Indies and Guiana, circa 1960, in terms of the legacy of four hundred years of European domination. The description of the Rastafarians gives pleasure. Their theology is based on the bible, exciting historical hypotheses—the present queen is the reincarnation of Elizabeth I, and Philip the reincarnation of her lover Philip IV of Spain—and stray copies of *The New York Times*. They believe that Trinidad is Hell (with some justification) and that Ethiopia's Haile Selassie I was the second coming of Christ. Christ was black but Christians have depicted him as white to suppress the truth and enhance their power.

BRITAIN AND ITS EMPIRE

The *Blackwell Classic Histories of England* (93) begin with the Saxon kings and run all the way to the present House of Windsor. They are excellent. Particularly touching was the last attempt of an English king—William IV—to rule as well as reign.

Charles Dickens portrays England just as the stage-coach gives way to rail and the country enters the industrial revolution. He has a lively sense of sympathy with its victims. That stuffed shirt Henry James thought him far too "sentimental"—more polite but akin to Nietzsche's reservations about Shakespeare being too close to the ill-smelling herd.

If you must read only two of Dickens' novels, try *A Tale of Two Cities* (94), which will give you an English perspective on the French Revolution, and *David Copperfield* (95), which is autobiographical. Dickens' mother, at a time when she was financially desperate, sent him to work in a shoe-dye factory, and when, a few months later, his father got out of debtors' prison, she wanted him to stay at work. He never forgave her. From childhood he dreamed of being a gentleman, and although he deplores the fact that Pip in *Great Expectations* becomes a snob, he never questions the class hierarchy of Britain.

America is the story of ethnicity and race and unusual

opportunities to make money. England tells something of the same story, but with opportunity less present and everything overlaid with class. Its upper classes, strange and aloof, never doubt their prerogatives. They co-opt some of the successful and others force entry, but within a generation most of these absorb the prevailing state of mind as naturally as breathing.

Howard Spring, *Fame is the Spur* (96) is worthwhile because of its moving account of the British working class at the end of the nineteenth century, and how they tried to better their lot in the twentieth. The sword of Peterloo is a symbol of their oppression: it was captured by a worker at the Peterloo massacre of August 1819, when British mounted troops used swords to cut down working people who had peacefully met to express their grievances. The book tells of the rise of the trade union movement, the Labour Party, and the suffragettes (and the vicious things that were done to them). There is a moving passage in which a trade union official, about to enjoy a cup of tea and fish paste on toast, suddenly thinks about how few of his neighbors can afford such luxuries. However, the most striking character is the protagonist, Hamer Shawcross, and the most striking thing about him is how easily he is co-opted by the upper class. He has no problem abandoning the cloth cap for the dinner party.

Cecil Woodham-Smith in *The Reason Why: The Story of the Fatal Charge of the Light Brigade* (97) tells how the aristocracy could buy the right to outfit a brigade and lead it into battle. But it is not just the suffering and the privilege that shock, it is the attitudes. There is reason to believe that the Light Brigade charged into the valley of death because Lord Cardigan misinterpreted the orders of Lord Lucan. Lord Cardigan was not speaking to Lord Lucan, and so would not humble himself to ask for clarification. In Barbara Tuchman, *The Proud Tower* (98) read the vignette on Keir Hardie. His employer dismisses him, a child of eight and the only member of his family in work. He does so surrounded by his own family enjoying a sumptuous breakfast, withholds the back pay the child is due, and lectures him on the evils of tardiness. (Hardie was late because he had walked miles through a driving rain.)

Tuchman has written a wonderful history of the early days of World War I, *The Guns of August* (99). The common cause of the war did not bridge the gulf that separated the classes. Lord Curzon, a leader in the War Cabinet, was surprised when he happened to observe British soldiers bathing: "How is it that I have never been informed that the lower orders have such white skins?" A pity the lower orders were useful as servants. Otherwise these strange white-skinned creatures could have been kept in zoos. These were the same people who could debate whether working class children of seven were damaged by crawling through mines pulling coal carts, and whether the Irish were actually dying of the "green mouth disease": they ate grass when they ran out of food.

R.H. Tawney, *The Acquisitive Society* (100) takes us into the twentieth century. He describes those who live among ordinary Britons as if surrounded by aborigines, and think nothing of the fact that they "wear several men's clothes, eat several men's dinners, occupy several families' houses, and live several men's lives." They see nothing odd about privilege without responsibility: Eton, Oxbridge, a club in town, London in June, the moors in August, pheasant shooting in October, Cannes in December, and hunting in February and March.

George Orwell in *The Road to Wigan Pier* (101) ranges broadly over the north during the Depression. ("Do you realize that people on the dole actually buy ice creams?") The north/south divide is still alive in England. The psychological barrier between the classes persists, although not as badly as during the 1970s. I met a worker who got top marks in a management course. After two such courses, he realized he was destined to take them forever. The firm simply did not know what to do with him: no one had ever moved from the shop floor to management. There were five tea rooms to insure that no class ever defiled another.

The English are masters of the comic novel. Evelyn Waugh wrote *Decline and Fall, Vile Bodies, A Handful of Dust, Scoop, Brideshead Revisited* and *The Loved One.* After *Brideshead Revisited* his serious novels got too serious as he became determined to proselytize for Catholicism.

In *Decline and Fall* (102), an architect views every home he designs with unspeakable disgust. The only creation that pleases him is a chewing-gum factory. He looks at a stairway: "Chewing-gum machines don't need stairs."

Kingsley Amis's *Lucky Jim* (103) is even better. Jim hesitates to enter a darkened room: his department head may be at a characteristic hobby, such as watching phosphorescent mould. When intoxicated, Jim gives a public lecture forced on him by his professor. His voice gradually approaches the tone of a Nazi at a book-burning reading excerpts from the work of a Jewish Communist author. Jim's 1950s' poverty illustrates how recently Britain achieved affluence. David Lodge in *Changing Places* (104) does the same with nice touches: the useless department head is revered because he did something in the war—no one is quite sure what.

Ian McEwan is one of the few decent writers to have won the Booker Prize, and his 2007 novel *On Chesil Beach* (105) works on many levels. It is about Edward and Florence, a couple very much in love, who fall apart because they are sexually naïve, untouched by the sexual revolution of the 1960s. The brief account of the life Edward was to lead thereafter is a snapshot of how the lives of ordinary Britons have altered from 1960 to the present. In an interview, McEwan mentioned taking a few pebbles from Chesil Beach to keep on his desk for inspiration. The Weymouth and Portland Borough Council threatened to fine him £2000, so he returned the pebbles.

There is England's Celtic fringe. Both Scots and Welsh people rather resent the image of their countries conveyed by *Decline and Fall,* Evelyn Waugh's comic novel noted earlier. Paul Pennyfeather is a divinity student expelled from Oxford for indecent exposure: his pants were removed by drunken young Scottish lairds who belonged to a social club that had, until recently, been banned because its members had stoned a fox to death with champagne bottles. He can get employment only in a Welsh day school, the headmaster of which has written a monograph with the theme that the Welsh have been known from time immemorial as unclean and have thus retained their racial purity. He also asserts they are the only group that has made no contribution to European civilization, save the blowing of dirges through silver-plated wind instruments. The local Welsh band is described as low of brow, and approaching with the loping tread of wolves.

Other novels are somewhat more sympathetic. Richard Llewellyn was born in England but had Welsh lineage and occasionally, if infrequently, visited Wales. His heart was located there and the result is a novel, *How Green Was My Valley* (106), that is pure poetry. Huw Morgan reminisces in very old age about the Welsh village of his youth as it was in the late nineteenth century. The valley gets less green as the slag heap from the coal mines grows. Owner versus union divides the valley. His father and older brother are killed. Indeed, by the time Huw leaves the valley everyone he loves has been killed or moved away. His sister is caught in a loveless marriage with a mine owner, and he has slept with his widowed sister-in-law (but can, of course, never marry her). The seduction scene is well written ("have you lost respect?"), contrasting favorably with the attempt of almost every contemporary novel to induce a sexual fantasy leading to near orgasm.

In Muriel Spark's *The Prime of Miss Jean Brodie* (107), Brodie is a teacher in Scotland in the 1930s. She lives through her control of a coterie of pupils: "Give me a girl at an impressionable age and she will be mine for life." She teaches them what she considers important—art, and admiration of Mussolini and Franco—and charts their lives, whether they are going to bed with one of her lovers or dying in Spain for the Fascists. The characters are drawn with impeccable skill. Graham Greene recognized Spark's talent before she was successful, and when she was recovering from dependence on amphetamines he gave her money to see her through.

Two novelists have each written a multi-volume series tracing English life over many decades. C.P. Snow's *Strangers and Brothers* is about Oxbridge intellectuals, but their lives reflect history between the two world wars and after. *The Masters* (108) is the best known book of the series: Old Gaye, who turns every common-room tea into a personal feast ("my compliments to the chef"), is a great character. But read *The Light and the Dark* (109). Roy Calvert, a charismatic young scholar cursed by manic depression, recovers the will to live just in time to die in World War II. If the last paragraph does not make you weep, something is wrong with you. Anthony Powell wrote

A Dance to the Music of Time, whose twelve volumes cover English political, cultural and military life over half a century. Read the first, *A Question of Upbringing* (110), in which the narrator begins to tell of his schooldays.

The trauma of twentieth-century England has been, as Orwell put it, the loss of an empire that left it a not very important island off the coast of Europe. By 1918 the sun had set on *all* the European empires, although it took their rulers fifty years to realize it. Today, only the United States thinks it can establish an empire. Exceptions are mainly English statesmen who desperately want to hold on to the coat-tails of an empire, even if it is somebody else's. They enjoy a "special relationship" with America. This means America gets almost automatic support for its foreign adventures at the trivial price of pretending, while laughing up its sleeve, that it pays attention to what prime ministers think.

Britain was the first nation into the industrial revolution. It had the naval tradition of an island nation. It could also sink most of its resources into its fleet because, unlike other European powers, it did not have to maintain a large army on the continent of Europe once it gave up its territorial ambitions there. That navy would not have been enough without two other assets: the country's sense of moral superiority, and the fact that so many Asian and Africa peoples were stunned into thinking they really were inferior. In addition, these peoples were still pre-nationalistic, and some were willing to side with the British for advantage against traditional local rivals. Britain's first colony was, of course, Ireland, and the struggle to get it out of Ireland is only now approaching closure.

For the insidious effects of imperialism, read Mahatma Gandhi, *An Autobiography: The Story of My Experiments with Truth* (111). Gandhi once believed that the English had a physical and inner strength his countrymen lacked and, despite being a Hindu, experimented with eating meat to see if that was their secret. An example of what the English thought is Rudyard Kipling's *Kim* (112), published in 1901. Kim is the orphan son of an Irish soldier. According to Kipling, that exempts him from the fate that awaits Indian boys: lively minds until adolescence, at which stage intellectual torpor, a sort of premature senility, sets in.

Two things swept away the psychology on which empire was built. First, the notion that Asians could not compete was shattered in 1905, when Japan beat Russia in a war. Europeans were astounded. Later, in 1942, despite numerical inferiority, the Japanese captured Singapore, the "Gibraltar of the East", from British troops and took 130,000 prisoners. They cheated: rather than a frontal attack by sea they came overland, riding bicycles. They also sunk two battleships, *Prince of Wales* and *Repulse*.

Secondly, the sense of moral superiority faded with the mindless slaughter in World War I. England and the other European powers were revealed to be members of a community of homicidal maniacs, unfit to run a hen house, much less the world. In the first months, the entire graduating class of the French military academy was killed. The American Civil War had proved that troops could not charge entrenched defenders using primitive rifles, yet World War I generals repeatedly tried mass charges against machine-guns. Perhaps, in retrospect, Haig decided to just get so many men killed that someone would run out of cannon fodder, preferably the Germans. Read A.H. Farrar-Hockley, *The Somme* (113). The battle lasted four and half months, from July 1 to November 19, 1916. There were 1,200,000 casualties.

Sebastian Faulks in *Birdsong* (114) tells how very terrible the war in the trenches was. Towards the end of the novel, a woman whose grandfather had fought visits the battlefield near Arras. There is an arch supported by four vast columns. Etched over hundreds and hundreds of yards of stone, furlongs of stone, there are names:

> *"Who are these, these? The men who died in this battle?"*
>
> *"No. The lost, the ones they did not find. The others are in the cemeteries."*
>
> *"These are just the ... the unfound." When she could speak again.*
>
> *"From the whole war?"*
>
> *The man shook his head. "Just these fields."*
>
> *Elizabeth sat on the steps. "No one told me. My God no one told me."*

Anyone who could think was dismayed: so our civilization comes down to this?

Young men would fight and die for their country again, but often it was a matter of dying for the lesser of two evils. Fortunately, Hitler was so evil he made this easy. Those still full of fervor wanted to overthrow European civilization. Something had collapsed within Europe's psyche. It was not just a matter of the enormous loss of life. America had lost a similar percentage of its young men in the Civil War, but there had been some point to it: slavery was abolished and the Union was saved. With its moral rudder intact, American entered into a post-war era of expansion and exuberance.

THE HUMAN CONDITION II

William Cowper, the late eighteenth-century poet, provides an example of the kind of certitude Britons had so long as they had religious faith. He thought that God had saved him from unforgivable sin: a sudden fog had prevented him from finding a river in which to drown himself. He wrote (so beautiful):

> God moves in a mysterious way
> His wonders to perform;
> He plants His footsteps in the sea
> And rides upon the storm.

In 1867, post Darwin and post faith, Matthew Arnold published *Dover Beach*:

> The Sea of Faith
> Was once, too, at the full, and round earth's shore
> Lay like the folds of a bright girdle furl'd.
> But now I only hear
> Its melancholy, long, withdrawing roar,
> Retreating, to the breath
> Of the night-wind, down the vast edges drear
> And naked shingles of the world.

Ah, love, let us be true
To one another! for the world, which seems
To lie before us like a land of dreams,
So various, so beautiful, so new,
Hath really neither joy, nor love, nor light,
Nor certitude, nor peace, nor help for pain;
And we are here as on a darkling plain
Swept with confused alarms of struggle and flight,
Where ignorant armies clash by night.

In 1920, post World War I, William Butler Yeats published *The Second Coming*:

Turning and turning in the widening gyre
The falcon cannot hear the falconer;
Things fall apart; the centre cannot hold;
The blood-dimmed tide is loosed, and everywhere
The ceremony of innocence is drowned;
The best lack all conviction, while the worst
Are full of passionate intensity.

A shape with lion body and the head of a man,
A gaze blank and pitiless as the sun,
Is moving its slow thighs, while all about it
Reel shadows of the indignant desert birds.
The darkness drops again; but now I know
That twenty centuries of stony sleep
Were vexed to nightmare by a rocking cradle,

And what rough beast, its hour come round at last,
Slouches towards Bethlehem to be born?

Arnold and Yeats were prescient. Between the wars, those filled with passionate sincerity would be the admirers of two maniacs whose ideals were based on racial myths (Hitler) and historical lies (Stalin). Soon enough, two "rough beasts" would be slouching towards Bethlehem to be born.

For those who wanted a better world, Arnold's affectionate ties with loved ones were not enough. Two men, Bertrand Russell and Aldous Huxley, typify the search for something more. Thanks to logical positivism and the philosophy of language, which left ideals to "preachers", British academics were of no help. They went to sleep until about 1950.

Ray Monk wrote a two-volume biography of Russell: *Bertrand Russell: The Spirit of Solitude 1872–1921* (115) and *Bertrand Russell: The Ghost of Madness 1921–1970*. Monk is too censorious. As my colleague and Russell scholar Charles Pigden says when reviewing his own conduct: a man is always at his worst when courting. Russell was trying to impress some woman or another throughout most of his long life.

Russell was dismayed to find that even mathematics gave no certitude, so what of ethics? Philosophy suggested it had no rational foundation at all. He devoted his life to causes he thought must be good if anything was: women's suffrage, opposition to World War I, nuclear disarmament. His activism, of course, provided no reasoned justification for the good. It is unclear whether Russell ever found anything that satisfied him. The closest he came was in his *History of Western Philosophy* (116), published in 1945. In it, he uses logic and evidence to criticize opponents of humane ideals such as Nietzsche. This was shortly after a United States court found him "morally unfit" to teach university students because of his unorthodox views on sex. He must have succeeded in corrupting them: not much later students were sleeping with everything but squirrels.

Russell writes philosophy as you have never seen it written. Do not be put off by the book's scholarly critics ("neglects the post-Cartesian period"). In addition, be sure to read his *Unpopular Essays* (117). You will particularly enjoy the chapter entitled "An Outline of Intellectual Rubbish": "Of China, Hegel knew only that it *was*, therefore China represented the category of mere Being."

Aldous Huxley tried to give ideals such as compassion and self-transcendence—which is to say ethics and "religion"—an empirical foundation. He felt this would make them the equal of science. His early novels do not take him far, but they are an education about the world of ideas and some are very funny.

In his Hollywood novel *After Many a Summer Dies the Swan* (118), he portrays a mogul who thinks evolving into a chimpanzee is a small price to pay if he can stay alive and have sex. ("They do look rather happy don't they.") Why he has to pay that price is made plausible. In *Point Counter Point* (119), Lord Edward opposes both fascism and communism because either would deplete the world's supply of phosphates. When told that without communism we will have wars and depopulate much of the Earth, his resolve is strengthened. At least there will be enough phosphates to go around.

Teachers will enjoy *Antic Hay* (120). Theodore Gumbril marks an exam question on Pope Pius IX. The pupils have been told that Pius IX declared the doctrine of papal infallibility and that, while well-intentioned, his policies were not shrewd. The answers come back: "Pope Pius IX was a kindly man but had less than average intelligence; therefore, he thought he was infallible." After the tenth answer, Gumbril gives up schoolteaching for a higher calling: he designs underwear with inflatable bottoms—"a comfort to all travelers."

Huxley's solutions to all problems—moral, spiritual, economic (large-scale industry to be abolished), the consumer society, exploitation and war—are given in a rather preachy novel, *Island* (121). Huxley's answer is pacifism, based on a simple society in which everyone can transcend the self through the mystical experience. I have no doubt the mystical experience is good for those who can have it—Huxley posits a fictitious drug that allows everyone to have it—but I do not believe it can bear the philosophical weight of justifying humane ideals and a godless substitute for religion.

Russell and Huxley differ from Fitzgerald. Fitzgerald was disappointed that America did not supply him with worthy ideals; Russell and Huxley realized it is up to each individual to find a commitment to humane ideals in their own heart. However, they also wanted something more, something that has deep roots in our civilization, a yearning that goes all the way back to Plato. They wanted humane ideals to be "true" and all others to be "false". They wanted humane ideals to have a superior status, based on logic or "science" (experience). They wanted to be able to show that anyone who does not hold humane ideals ought to do so, in the sense that, if they do not, they can be convicted of some sin against reason—such as being guilty of a logical contradiction, or ignoring some special way of discovering what is really right and wrong, or misunderstanding human nature. Without this, humane ideals were somehow downgraded. They became mere convictions, relevant only to those with a particular psychology—namely, those who happened to care about people in general.

My own "solution" to this problem (in Part IV of *Where Have All the Liberals Gone?)* is that there is no such thing as knowledge of good and evil, and we would not like it if there were. I believe there are six great goods: the general happiness, justice, truth, beauty, delight in human diversity, and the integrity of human nature. And every time someone has offered a case that humane ideals are objective or true, they end up ranking these six great goods in a way that is repugnant—for example, they force us to always put the happiness of humankind ahead of justice, or always put justice ahead of the happiness of humankind. Things are more complicated than that. Moreover, even without a case for the truth of my ideals, I can often show that my opponents say things that are clearly false. For example, racists have to say things we all know to be false about Jewish or black people.

I may be mistaken of course. People must make up their own minds about these issues. The novels of John Barth listed in the first section on the human condition will give you a good start. But eventually you will have to read some moral philosophy.

GERMANY, FRANCE AND RUSSIA

To see Europe in medieval times, read Barbara Tuchman, *A Distant Mirror* (122). Here I cannot improve on the blurb from Wikipedia. The book covers the cataclysms suffered by Europe in the fourteenth century: the Hundred Years' War, the Black Plague, the papal schism, pillaging mercenaries and popular revolts, the liberation of Switzerland, and peasant uprisings against laws that enforced the use of hops in beer. Tuchman takes care to describe the lives of the people, from nobles and clergymen, right down to the peasantry. Other than this book, my recommendations focus on the modern era.

GERMANY

Erich Maria Remarque fought in World War I and hated German militarism. He married the Hollywood actress Paulette Goddard in 1958. They were very much in love throughout the twelve years he had left. The Nazis burned his books and claimed that he was a descendant of a Jew named Kramer, which name he had taken to spelling backwards. In 1943, frustrated that he was living in America, they found his sister guilty of treason—she was overheard saying that the war was lost—and cut off her head.

Remarque's novels give a wonderful account of Germany during and between the wars. His most famous is *All Quiet on the Western Front* (123) but the subsequent ones are even better. You must read four. *The Black Obelisk* (124) describes the era when inflation made money worthless. The title refers to the tombstone industry, which was flourishing due to the large number of suicides. The whole structure of middle-class life was under threat. The domineering father who controlled his daughter by providing a dowry could no longer provide one. If the wife could barter eggs, it was more important than the husband's wage. A family who had saved for years to send a child to university found that their savings melted away. My old professor, Hans Morgenthau, once told me that all the money saved by his family for his four years at university dwindled so much over one summer that it would not pay even a month's board. The German virtues of hard work, thrift and prudence were now ludicrous. All of this came on the heels of the humiliation of having lost World War I. The publisher's blurb for *The Black Obelisk* calls it the best book of the twentieth century. A reader exclaims, "If I ever tire of reading this book, I will know I am tired of life."

In *Three Comrades* (125), you have a wonderful love story, but also an account of what the Depression, the joblessness of the 1930s, did to Germany. It was these three blows—the lost war, inflation and the Depression—in quick succession that turned so many Germans from people into Nazis.

The German war experience is portrayed in *A Time to Love and a Time to Die* (126). A soldier returns home from the Russian front, where things are unpleasant. (If you wrench off a frozen boot, you find the flesh comes with it, leaving you looking at the bones of your foot.) He loves a young woman whose father is in a concentration camp. The labor camps (not the extermination camps) are described in *Spark of Life* (127). It is so moving that you can hardly bear to turn the pages.

Remarque is not the only novelist who can acquaint you with twentieth-century Germany. Heinrich Mann was the elder brother of Thomas Mann. The Nazis hated him, but fortunately he sneaked across the French border on the day the police came to his apartment to arrest him. The excellent film *The Blue Angel* is based on one of his novels, and although Hitler banned the film it is said he viewed it in private. He liked Marlene Dietrich. Heinrich Mann's most important novel *The Loyal Subject* (or *Man of Straw*) is not to my taste. There is too much tedious detail. Nonetheless, although published in 1918, a year before the Nazi party was founded, it does a remarkable job of capturing the psychology of Germans who were just waiting for someone like Hitler to recruit them. Anti-Semitism is everywhere, even among a few Jews who are ambitious and want to assimilate. There are liberals who ostensibly would be resistant, but their liberalism is only skin deep. They are infected almost as much as the far right by nation worship and force worship.

Thomas Mann is such a good writer that I enjoy him despite a certain formality of style. You get the impression he is well aware of his genius. He is capable of plain good writing and you will enjoy the sheer artistry of *Death in Venice* (128) and his comic novel *The Confessions of Felix Krull, Confidence Man.*

His masterpiece is *The Magic Mountain* (129). He said that to fully comprehend its depths you had to read the book twice, but that is unnecessary unless you are obsessed with time, the relation of time to space, why the mountain is said to be magical, and so forth. Especially avoid reading Mann's analysis of what the novel means. Enjoy it for its characterizations, and the wonderful picture it gives of cosmopolitan European society in the early twentieth century. A diverse group of people are patients in a tuberculosis sanatorium in the Alps. Some are terrified of death. Others are brave, or commit suicide. The main character survives to go off to World War I, probably to be killed. The book poses a question that is worth pondering: how did such a civilized society produce such a barbaric war? The portrayals of two characters in particular, Naphta and Ziemssen, are enlightening.

If you want to know why Germans who were children in World War I threw themselves with such enthusiasm into World War II, see Sebastian Haffner's memoir *Defying Hitler* (130). The war never touched the children directly (Germany surrendered prior to invasion) and the war news was the most thrilling thing to relieve the tedium of their school lives. They were like soccer fanatics awaiting the scores that would show how well their team had done. And all the news was of victories—until the inexplicable surrender at the end.

Christopher Isherwood wrote two novels about Germany between the wars: *Goodbye to Berlin* (131), which introduces the "divinely decadent" Sally Bowles, and *Mr Norris Changes Trains* (132). Sally Bowles and her friends travel widely. They include a Jewish woman and two gay men; all will soon be under threat from Hitler. *Goodbye to Berlin* was adapted to make two great films, *I Am A Camera*, which has some good comedy, and *Cabaret*. One scene from the latter is especially powerful. A German aristocrat in the group has been saying that Hitler can be easily controlled. They arrive at a beer garden and a beautiful blonde boy in a Hitler Youth uniform begins singing "Tomorrow Belongs to Me". (This was not a Nazi song, but composed for the film.) The whole crowd is swept away and joins in the singing, except two men who are obviously workers (cloth caps) and either socialists or communists. The group says to their aristocratic friend, "And you think you can control him?" Mr Norris is a communist spying for France under Hitler: all of his comrades are killed but he escapes to Argentina. He is not so sure he is lucky.

Before his liberation by the Russians in January 1945, Primo Levi, an Italian Jew, spent a year in the extermination camp at Auschwitz. You worked until it was your turn to die. His description of his life there in *If This is a*

Man (133) and of his long journey home to Italy in *The Truce* are a continuous story, normally published as a single volume. His account is all the more effective because of his beautiful unadorned prose. Despite his "optimism" that it was possible to remain a human being even in hell, he was troubled by his experiences throughout his life. It is hotly debated whether his death forty years later was an accident or suicide. Among the inmates, the Greek Jews from Salonika stand out for their unbelievable toughness, solidarity, and skill at theft. Theft was endemic: if your hands were occupied, you had to clamp your possessions between your knees.

During World War II there was resistance to Hitler, however futile, at all levels of society, from the aristocracy to camp inmates. Some Germans did virtually suicidal things on principle. For example, a philosophy professor and his pupils—the White Rose group—circulated leaflets calling for active resistance and six were beheaded. A few died thinking their execution would inspire other students to act, but the rest had no such hope. They simply felt they could not stand by and do nothing.

There is one book in particular that will keep you from demonizing all Germans. During the Nazi era, Hans Fallada was in and out of prison and was a morphine addict. At the war's end, he wrote *Every Man Dies Alone* (134) in twenty-four days. He died two months later. In the book he describes horrible people who delight in inform-ing on their neighbors, but also gives a fictionalized account of the actual case of a humble working-class couple. After the wife's brother is killed in the war (in the novel this becomes their son), the couple leave postcards denouncing Hitler in office buildings and are subsequently executed. They make only one convert: a detective who apprehends them cannot face what he has become in the process, and commits suicide. Other heroes emerge: a former judge who hides a Jewish woman, and a woman who hides fugitives at her flat. All are dead by the end, save one lucky woman who hides in a rural area and begins to rear a former member of Hitler Youth to be a decent person.

FRANCE

Nineteenth-century France is portrayed in the works of three great novelists. In *Les Misérables* (135), Victor Hugo covers from Waterloo in 1815 through the Paris uprising of 1832. The hero, Jean Valjean, has served nineteen years of hell for stealing a loaf of bread and is being now pursued for a trivial crime. Over 1200 pages, Hugo tells us why Napoléon lost, the history of anti-monarchism in France, and about the decay of the church. The Bernardine nuns did not allow toothbrushing. Martin Verga had made the rules some centuries earlier; he was a stern man.

In *The Kill* (136), Émile Zola contrasts the dishonesty of the rich who finance the rebuilding of Paris with the workers who do the work. Rich men, chatting about the uselessness of the lower classes, look up to see a man risking his life on a crane high above the street: "But, I say, that fellow does have pluck, doesn't he." In *Germinal* (137), visitors to a mine see a huge horse and ask how it gets in and out. The horse came down as a little foal, never to leave save at death, a powerful image of the men themselves.

On January 13, 1898, Zola wrote the most famous newspaper article in history: "J'accuse". The military had framed a Jew, Alfred Dreyfus, for treason and imprisoned him on Devil's Island. The case tore France apart: see Paul Johnson's *A History of the Jews*. Zola died at sixty-two of poisoning caused by a stopped chimney. Decades later, a dying man claimed he had closed the chimney for political reasons. Anti-Semitism lives on in France today.

Gustave Flaubert loved an older woman who was in and out of insane asylums. His *Madam Bovary* (138) is a great novel. Henry James called Emma Bovary a contemptible trollop (enough from him). Read Flaubert's *Sentimental Education* (139); it so enamored the youth of his day that they memorized the entire 400 pages. This may have exhausted them in that they wrote nothing much themselves. The book contrasts revolutionaries, the middle class and the rich against the backdrop of the revolution of 1848. (The French have an affinity for revolutions.) What Flaubert thought of the élite: "They would have sold France or the whole human race to safeguard their fortune, to spare themselves the slightest feeling of discomfort or embarrassment, or even out of mere servility and worship of strength." My edition says the book shows up French

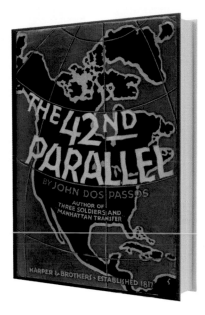

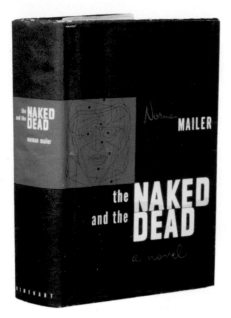

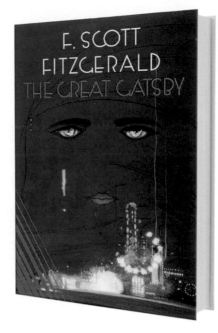

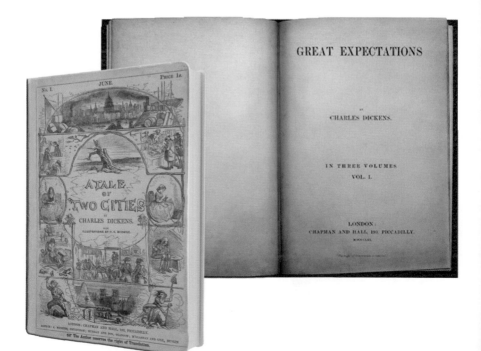

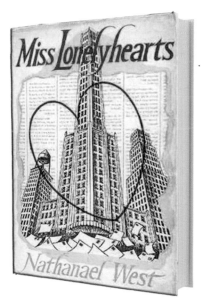

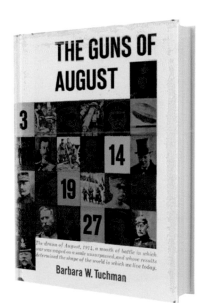

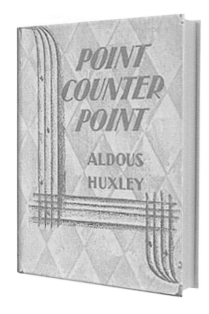

POINT
COUNTER
POINT

ALDOUS
HUXLEY

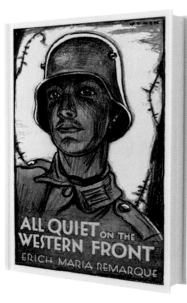

ALL QUIET ON THE
WESTERN FRONT
ERICH MARIA REMARQUE

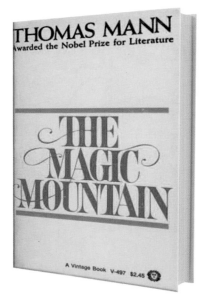

THOMAS MANN
Awarded the Nobel Prize for Literature

THE
MAGIC
MOUNTAIN

A Vintage Book   V-497 $2.45

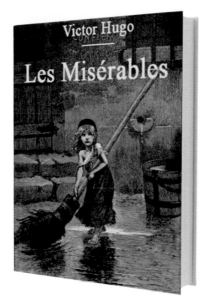

Victor Hugo

Les Misérables

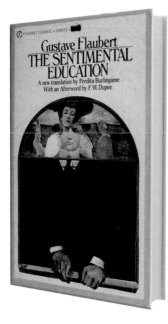

A SIGNET CLASSIC • CW579 •

Gustave Flaubert
THE SENTIMENTAL
EDUCATION
A new translation by Perdita Burlingame
With an Afterword by F. W. Dupee

THEATRE DU CHATELET

GERMINAL

ÉMILE ZOLA

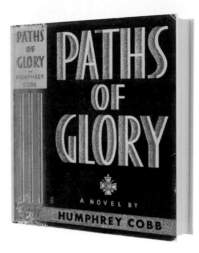

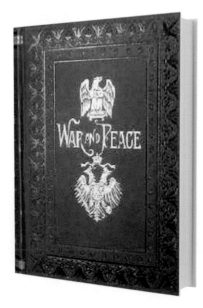

ARTHUR KOESTLER

Darkness

at

Noon

ARTHUR KOESTLER

Author of
The Gladiators, Spanish Testament, etc.

$2.45

NORTON CRITICAL EDITIONS

FFODOR DOSTOEVSKY

Crime and Punishment

THE COULSON TRANSLATION
BACKGROUNDS AND SOURCES
ESSAYS IN CRITICISM

EDITED BY GEORGE GIBIAN

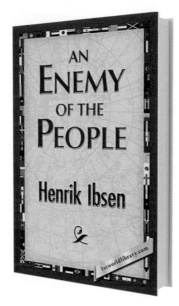

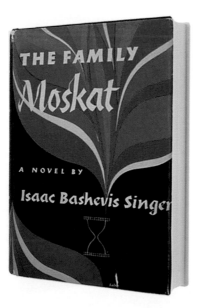

politics of the twentieth century as much as those of the nineteenth. I never met a Frenchman, other than a politician, who disagreed. Jean-Paul Sartre wrote a four-volume biography of Flaubert showing that he was merely a product of his time. Sadly, Flaubert could not return the favor.

Humphrey Cobb was born in Italy and fought in World War I with the Canadian army. Despite this, many French found that *Paths of Glory* (140) depicted their disillusion. If you have a chance, see the 1957 film with Kirk Douglas and Adolphe Menjou. The troops are ordered to attack a hopelessly strong position, and enemy fire throws them back into their trenches. The general needs a scapegoat. Since he cannot shoot a whole battalion, he orders the execution of one hundred, to be chosen by lot. Thanks to his humanity, he is persuaded to reduce the number to three. The troop commander argues that he should be the one shot if anyone is. But this is unthinkable because he is an officer.

During World War II, Hitler made moral choice clear: he unleashed a plague of bestiality and barbarism and you were either for him or against him. In 1947, Albert Camus captured the situation in his novel *The Plague* (141). You need not read it as an allegory to enjoy it. The bubonic plague hits the Algerian city of Oran and medical workers unite to fight it. The diverse reactions of people ranging from residents to visitors to fugitives are described with subtlety. The main character concludes that, on balance, people are worth saving. At the very end we are reminded that the respite is temporary: the plague will come again.

After the war, there was the usual moral uncertainty: what ideals, if any, are worthwhile? In addition, the terrible war between France and the Algerian rebels seemed a declaration of moral bankruptcy.

Sartre tried to fill the void with existentialism. We become "authentic" by creating selves, rather than allowing convention to make us in its image. This seems to me a truism rather than very helpful. The existentialists are equally unappreciative of my work. Asked for a critique of an analytic philosopher, a French philosopher said, "He is a cow." This is not the best put-down in the history of philosophy. My favorite is William James' comment about his colleague Josiah Royce: One had only to look at him to know he had invented a new proof of the existence of God. Google his photo and you will appreciate what James meant. Sartre did write one good play. *No Exit* portrays Hell as three people who get on each other's nerves but have to spend eternity together in a hotel room.

The Algerian war blighted France from 1954 to 1962. It is hard to tell who was the most brutal: the French army, the colon (French settlers who looked upon Algeria as home), or the Algerian nationalists (who wanted independence, and the colon to leave). In late November 1960, General Charles de Gaulle, now president, began to implement a policy that would give Algeria independence. France was being torn apart. Sartre, and Catholics such as Jacques Maritain, urged young Frenchmen to refuse to fight. The army planned a coup d'état, soldiers were brutalized by having to carry out torture, and massacres became endemic. The atmosphere is vividly portrayed in Frederick Forsyth's best novel *The Day of the Jackal* (142), about a professional assassin who is contracted by a French terrorist group to assassinate de Gaulle.

RUSSIA

Leo Tolstoy fought in the Crimean War and liked wearing military uniforms, but later became a pacifist who influenced both Gandhi and Martin Luther King. His *War and Peace* (143) has 580 characters and a sweep rivaled only by the work of Isaac Bashevis Singer. Its focus is Russia's defeat of Napoléon in 1812. It covers the generals and the tsar, the battles, and why Russian society was far more significant than "great men".

The opening lines of *Anna Karenina* (144) will convince you of how well Tolstoy could write: "Happy families are all alike; every unhappy family is unhappy in its own way." Literary critics focus on the fact that trains are present throughout the novel, although they have to count the fact that children are playing with toy trains in the first few chapters. Avoid such people. The novel is about family, marriage and society in nineteenth-century Russia, and the gulf between the life of the peasants and that of the city dwellers.

Nikolai Gogol died when he went mad and refused to eat. This was despite the best medical attention of the day: they attached leeches to his nose. *Dead Souls* (145) portrays Russian under serfdom, which was not abolished until 1861. Serfs could be bought and sold and were referred to as "souls". Gogol himself did not oppose serfdom, but to a modern eye the serf owners were a class long overdue for being discarded into the dustbin of history. One is a swindler, another mad, a third a miser, a fourth a totally demoralised idler. The absurd values and etiquette of small-town pre-revolutionary Russian society are laid bare: the protagonist and his host are barely capable of entering a room because each refuses to precede the other.

Ivan Turgenev wrote *Fathers and Sons* (146) in 1862. It contrasts the older generation, traditionalists, with the new younger generation, who called themselves nihilists— the old order had to be scrapped. Turgenev rejected mere spirituality, and Tolstoy challenged him to a duel. It did not take place but the two did not speak for seventeen years. He admired Gogol: "Gogol is dead. . . . What Russian heart is not shaken by those three words?" For publishing this, he was imprisoned for a month, and then exiled to his country estate for two years.

Alexander Pushkin did die in a duel (with his wife's alleged lover). He ruined himself by gambling, and his short story "The Queen of Spades" is about a man obsessed with the secret of three cards that always guarantee a win. He ends in an asylum, where "he doesn't answer any questions and he keeps muttering with extraordinary rapidity, 'Three, seven, ace! Three, seven, queen!'"

Perhaps you sense there is something odd about Russian intellectuals. It is called the Russian soul. Anton Chekhov's play *The Seagull* (147) shows that some kind of romantic weirdness was not confined to a few. "The Russian Novel" is a wonderful short story that captures the Russian psyche. A young woman remarks that her parents are concerned about her little brother: "He is already four and has not yet attempted suicide." I thought this story was by the comic writer James Thurber (do read his collection *92 Stories*) but it is not. My gratitude to any reader who can locate it for me.

Twentieth-century Russian history is about the revolution of 1917, its culmination in the tyranny of Joseph Stalin, and the aftermath in the post-Communist era. Stalin's paranoia was such that he executed all his old comrades—one was accused of concealing swastikas in a design on teacups—and sent millions to their deaths. He did do a reasonable job (eventually) of repulsing the Nazi invasion of Russia in World War II.

Stalin's 1938 show trials were famous for the fact that people kept confessing in court to fantastic crimes without bearing obvious marks of torture. Arthur Koestler in *Darkness at Noon* (148) gives a plausible scenario. The interrogator convinces Rubashov, an old Bolshevik being tried for treason, that Stalin is historically necessary. He may be insane, but who but a madman would have been willing to kill all the people who had to be killed to modernize Russia? Peasants would straggle into work as late as they pleased, and the railway needed would not be built. Shoot some and they came on time.

Aleksandr Solzhenitsyn wrote *The Gulag Archipelago*, a three-volume book about the huge forced labor system under Stalin; he himself had been a prisoner in a Gulag labor camp. The book traces the history of the Soviet concentration camp from 1918 to 1956, ending with Nikita Khrushchev's secret speech to the Twentieth Congress of the Community Party denouncing Stalin's personality cult. That speech is odd. It gives the impression there was this evil magician called Stalin who somehow got power by waving a wand. Marxists are supposed to think sociologically: a corrupt ruler can emerge only from a corrupted society. But that would have posed the embarrassing question of what social movement did the corrupting. I have not numbered this work because you may wish to take the easier path of reading two of Solzhenitsyn's novels: *One Day in the Life of Ivan Denisovich* (149) and *The First Circle* (150).

Stalin subjugated Eastern Europe from 1945 to 1989. Czesław Miłosz, *The Captive Mind* (151) is a wonderful book about what it was like to be an intellectual in Poland at that time—aware of the awfulness of what was going on, but having to rationalize the role you played. A man called a swine by émigrés to the West thinks of how much harder it is to have stayed behind and fought for small victories than to go to New York and call people swine. Miłosz was a poet, and even in translation the book reads like poetry. The section on Delta, the troubadour, is particularly affecting. He is a child-like man who writes for the masses, and therefore tries to please any ruler who gives him access to a wide audience. Under Piłsudski, the pre-war dictator of Poland, he would write anti-Semitic verses and then call on his Jewish friends, bringing gifts and drunkenly begging their forgiveness. Under the Communists, he tries to please but he is too spontaneous and naïve to know how. He is doomed.

After Miłosz defected from Communist Poland to the United States, he found himself under suspicion because he was a Democratic Socialist. America was wary: if they call themselves "Socialists", arc they not some kind of communist? This is despite the fact that Socialists were often the first to be jailed by Stalinist regimes.

Milan Kundera is a Czech writer with an international readership. In his book *The Joke* (152), Ludvik Jahn is a student who supports the new Communist regime. In a postcard he facetiously says, "Optimism is the opium of the people." The interrogation he faces afterwards is both chilling and absurd. The fact he was joking merely shows he believes that the optimism of those inspired by the new regime is a joke. Does he think that building communism is a joking matter? This one misstep alters his life. He is expelled, sent to work in the mines, and becomes a cynical outsider.

Kundera himself, although fully aware of the flaws of the regime, hoped for reform: even after 1968, when Russia crushed the democratic reforms of Alexander Dubček, he noted that he and other critics were not imprisoned. He finally abandoned his country for France in 1975.

In 1989, the fall of the Berlin Wall that kept people from fleeing to the West signaled the end of communist rule in Eastern Europe. The best book about the Soviet Union at that time is Hedrick Smith's *The Russians* (153). Smith crossed the country by train (no doubt that is deeply significant) and interviewed dissidents, officials and ordinary people. By 1991 communism was collapsing in the Soviet Union itself. In *Goodnight, Mister Lenin* (154), the Italian journalist Tiziano Terzani records his impressions of nearly all the new nations now more or less free from Russian domination. He interviews minorities who are uncomfortable in these new states, rebels who are now state leaders, emerging young criminals, and some Cossacks who entrust him with a letter to the Pope.

THE HUMAN CONDITION III

In *The Brothers Karamazov* (155), Fyodor Dostoyevsky asks what ethics means in a godless universe. This is the *third* time we have been invited to ask how we can justify humane ideas. It is the great philosophical problem of our time.

There are four brothers. Alyosha—named after Dostoyevsky's son, who died at the age of three—has religious faith. Ivan is a skeptic. He tells his half-brother, Smerdyakov, that without faith anything is allowable. Smerdyakov then proceeds to kill their father to prove he really does believe anything is allowable. He gives Ivan the credit: "You murdered him; you are the real murderer. I was only your instrument, your faithful servant, and it was following your words I did it." Ivan is dismayed: he did not expect to be taken so literally. Dmitry, the fourth brother, is mistakenly accused and put on trial. Asked if he believes in God, he replies that he has come to believe: there is so much evil in the world there must be a devil, and if there is a devil there must be a god. Few readers have found this proof of the existence of God sufficient to restore their religious faith.

Dostoyevsky prepared us for his theme in an earlier novel, the wonderful *Crime and Punishment* (156). Like Smerdyakov, Raskolnikov is motivated by secular rationalism. He kills a pawnbroker (with an axe) in her apartment, and also has to kill her half-sister, who happens to make an untimely visit. He anticipates Nietzsche's message that if God is dead we are beyond good and evil. Supermen have the right to use herd men as mere means to great purposes. Several times during the novel, Raskolnikov justifies his actions by likening himself to Napoléon, who got millions slaughtered so as to remake Europe. It should be said that Nietzsche would have despised Raskolnikov, who has no great purpose and is incurably moralistic: he wants the pawnbroker's money, and keeps condemning her as a useless parasite profiting from the misery of others. Nietzsche had no objection to useless parasites clever enough to exploit others.

There are some wonderful minor characters. Katerina beats her children mercilessly, but works tirelessly to show that she and her family are not mere slum dwellers. Following her husband's death, she wastes Raskolnikov's money on an ostentatious funeral. Her daughter, Sonya, is a prostitute driven to her profession by her mother's rage and her family's penury. She is full of Christian virtue. Russian novelists are always inventing characters like that.

Dostoyevsky is even more tortured than F. Scott Fitzgerald and Bertrand Russell by the problem of what ideals are worthy of commitment. No doubt that is because he has a Russian soul. The French are also emotional about the problem of ideals, which they call the "existential predicament". Their concern is diluted by the fact they know the purpose of life: good food. Recently a French chef found that if you soak a tomato in sugar long enough it begins to taste like sugar, and can be served as a dessert. This is called Gallic genius.

Some of Dostoyevsky's anguish is, I think, based on bad reasoning. He believes that if God does not vouch for our ideals, they are reduced to no more than casual whims. I am not religious and would put it differently: if we cannot make some sort of rational case that our ideals are worthy of regard from all mankind, they are personal commitments.

But there is a huge difference between the two. Simply because my ideals are based on my commitment to them does not mean they are no more important to me than my whims. Those of us in the American civil rights movement fifty years ago did not, when seeing someone choose to throw a little black girl through a plate-glass window, feel quite the same as when we saw someone choose to drink Coca-Cola rather than lemonade. In other words, we were willing to risk serious penalties for our ideal of racial equality; we would not have risked much of anything to defend our taste in soft drinks.

Dostoyevsky would accuse me of missing the point. If there is no voucher for the truth or objectivity of my ideals, I *ought* to treat them as no more than casual whims, and the fact I would find this difficult to do just shows how agonizing the problem is. I believe his conclusion is based on a logical mistake, which I call the nihilist fallacy. Where there is a truth test of some sort, it shows that my beliefs are either worthy of regard from everyone, or worthy of regard from no one, including myself. For example, if I am lost in a desert suffering from thirst and think I see an oasis in the distance, I can test the truth of my belief. If I run forward and scoop up "water" from the pool, I either get a mouthful of water (in which case the existence of the oasis is true for everyone) or a mouthful of sand (in which case the oasis is a mere mirage for everyone, including me).

So, when there is a test of the truth of my beliefs, they can flunk it and be discredited. But if there is no test in ethics, my ideals cannot pass or fail. If there is no test, how could anything fail? Dostoyevsky's mistake is to treat the absence of a test as equivalent to all human ideals having failed a test. Thus, he thinks all ideals are unworthy of regard, even from those who are deeply committed to them. This is nonsense: if there is no test, no ideal can be either exalted or discredited. No ideal is "true" in the sense that all must hold it whether they are committed to it or not, and no ideal is "false" in the sense that no one can hold it, whether they are committed to it or not.

Commitment reigns supreme. Your ideals are worth what they are worth to you. If you are committed to humane ideals, I hope they are worth a great deal to you. If you are committed to some anti-humane ideal—say, that those who lose in market competition are the "unfit"—I hope such ideals are not worth much to you.

But from sad experience I know they may be. Neither of us can show that the other's ideals are a mirage, or "hallucinatory". We will both fight for them and that is that.

To sum up: great works of literature from many nations force us to think about what our ideals mean in an age of godlessness and materialism. But novelists are not necessarily good moral philosophers. Whether humane ideals survive into the modern age depends on you.

Perhaps it is time to grow up morally. As Thornton Wilder said, there is a glory in forging our ideals within ourselves. Why give away our moral autonomy to a book, or put commitment at the mercy of an impartial method of obtaining "truth" that cares nothing for humane ideals? At one time, art and religion were so interwoven it was difficult for people to imagine painting without a religious theme. Throughout history, morality and a lawgiver—either God or a higher court of appeal that told us which morality was the true one—have been conjoined. As a result, thinkers, from Dostoyevsky to the moral realists of today, find it difficult to imagine that ethics can survive without them. Here is where learning the history of ideas through reading helps. We learn that certain attitudes about good were once so endemic that few could fail to internalize them. This allows us to free ourselves from similar attitudes. I am convinced that if I cannot do good based on my commitment to humane ideals, this tells the world something about me, rather than something eternal about morality.

SPAIN, PORTUGAL, ITALY AND SCANDINAVIA

France, Germany and Russia dominated Europe in turn in modern times, but the rest of the continent has a rich literature and a rich history. I have already insulted Eastern Europe by referring to it only during its period of Soviet occupation. Now I must offend the Balkans (even Greece), Switzerland, the Netherlands and Belgium by omitting them entirely. I have two good reasons: ignorance of their literature, and the fact the nations I cover in this chapter have been more influential, both historically and in their impact on European literature in general.

SPAIN AND PORTUGAL

Throughout the Middle Ages, Spain was preoccupied with eliminating Islamic control of her territory. By 1250 the major battles were over and Granada, the last Moorish state, had been reduced to a tributary. Spain was the greatest power in Europe with a world empire during the fifteenth and sixteen centuries. This was also the heyday of Portugal, which, despite being much smaller, acquired an empire of its own. These two countries divided all of Latin America between them, Portugal getting Brazil and Spain the rest.

Eventually, Spain and Portugal were eclipsed by nations quicker to industrialize, and religious intolerance robbed both of many of their most productive citizens. In 1478, Spain instituted the Inquisition. Jews had to flee or convert. Protestants and Jews suspected of being merely pro forma Christians were burned at the stake.

Spain undertook the burden of acting as defender of the Catholic faith in Europe. In the late seventeenth century, it waged a disastrous war to salvage Catholicism in the Netherlands, and this marked the beginning of the country's real decline. In the early nineteenth century, it suffered the humiliation of foreign armies fighting on its territory, and by 1898 it had lost most of its empire. During the latter half of the nineteenth century, monarchies and republics alternated without any real change, partly because the Spanish civil service remained unaltered: it had an extraordinary capacity to do nothing except exhaust public revenues to pay its salaries and perks.

In 1931, a real republic that was left-leaning was established. In 1936 General Franco, leading an army based in Spanish Morocco, invaded Spain and began a murderous civil war. With help from Hitler and Mussolini, he triumphed in 1939 and was dictator until his death in 1975, after which the country evolved a parliamentary democracy. From about 1960, Spain began a period of economic growth that abolished most of the terrible poverty, particularly in rural areas, that had burdened her history.

Richard Zimler moved from America to Portugal over twenty years ago. In *The Last Kabbalist of Lisbon* (157), he recounts the 1506 Lisbon massacre of Jews. He focuses on a Jew whose likely murderer was a "new Christian"— a converted Jew. By 1550, the Protestant Reformation has reached Spain. Miguel Delibes in *The Heretic* (158) tells the story of a group of Protestants who are discovered and burnt at the stake. Cipriano Salcedo is one of them. He is a progressive manufacturer, an exception in a city "where the highest aspiration of the poor is to fill their stomachs and the highest aspiration of the rich is to live off their rents." More than half the town is infected with syphilis; even street children are covered with sores and tumors. It makes vivid the climate of a time when any thinking person was obsessed with what God really required for salvation.

Spain's greatest nineteenth-century novelist is Benito Pérez Galdós. In *The Disinherited* (159), a woman obsesses that she has been denied recognition of her noble birth. Actually it is all of Spain that is disinherited. Its former greatness gone, its people do nothing except live beyond their means and swindle the public purse; indeed, not one character gives life purpose by cultivating a talent or trying to accomplish anything.

That Bringas Woman (160) plays variations on the same theme. Because Galdós is a nineteenth-century novelist, you must allow him time to set scene and character. For example, he spends three pages describing an absurdly intricate memorial piece that one of the main characters is making out of hair. This brilliant device captures the man's nature: he is a pedant who can think of nothing to do with his life except waste it on trivia. Galdós's masterpiece is said to be his long novel *Fortunata and Jacinta*. There are some good observations, but I did not find it as consistently interesting as his shorter novels.

He is a master of the telling phrase. The wife of a civil servant says: "He used to go into the office nearly every day and would often spend at least two hours there." On gentility: "As each one is furiously determined to go up in the world, he begins by posing"; "He was the finest man in the world, he was good for nothing"; "She received [the Marques] half dead with emotion and spoke to him with a trembling voice." Street children: one looks "like the Christ Child dressed as a bullfighter"; "If filth were an official decoration, the names of those young children would take up the whole of the Honours list"; they spoke "slang phrases that remind one of an ugly bee when it comes droning out of a lily." One child kills another. Planning commissions are formed to improve their lot: "They worked so well that in a short time there arose, all red and brutal, the new bull ring."

I cannot resist quoting one sentence: "Don Manuel José Ramón del Pez, indispensable on committees, needed on councils, the finest mind on Earth for speeding up or slowing down any matter, the best hand for drafting conditions for a loan, the most sensitive nose for smelling out a business transaction, servant of himself and others, encyclopedia of political witticisms, indefatigable apostle of venerable customs upon which rests the noble edifice of our national apathy, a machine for making laws, fashioning regulations, hacking out orders and molding instructions, the greatest milker ever to pull the udders of the country's exchequer, a man, to sum it up, whom you and I know like the back of our hand, more an era than a person, and rather than a personality he is a caste, a tribe, half Madrid, the symbol and epitome of half Spain."

You will understand one thing at least from reading Galdós: why nineteenth-century liberals thought that government best that governs least. The national budget is no more than a well-stocked cafeteria that serves up dishes to the privileged.

In 1936, George Orwell left England to fight for the republic against Franco in the Spanish Civil War. The most touching part of *Homage to Catalonia* (161) is the description of how people in Barcelona treated one another as equals. The workers had abolished tipping (well, New Zealand has got something right), and servile forms of speech such as "Señor" and "Don" had been abandoned. Rather than officers giving orders, "experienced comrades" (the few professional soldiers) give "instruction" to the ranks. Orwell served in a militia organized by an anti-Stalinist party. The Spanish Communists wanted complete control of the military and declared his unit an illegal organization. He was forced to flee, and left Spain a "convinced Democratic Socialist". Because of his book's criticism of the Communists, Victor Gollancz, who had published all of Orwell's previous books, rejected it. Orwell also wrote two great books against Stalinism: *1984* (162) and *Animal Farm* (163) ("all animals are equal but some are more equal than others").

A young man named Sidney from my neighborhood went to fight in Spain and died. About that time, all of the local couples on the left had girls, but that did not stop them from trying to immortalize his name, so if you meet a woman born in the 1930s in Washington, D.C. and her name is Sidney (like my wife's sister), you will know that her parents were left-wing. How is that for a piece of useless information?

Franco's victory in 1939 ushered in thirty-six years of dictatorship. Camilo José Cela fought on Franco's side in the civil war, but must have done so as the lesser of two evils because he has no illusions about the Spain that emerged. His first two novels are about life during World War II. (Spain was neutral.) If you have forgotten what it is like to be depressed, read them. *The Family of Pascual Duarte* (164) describes how the utterly barren rural Spain of the time generates a sociopath—not a sophisticated one who verbalizes his contempt for morality, but a brute unaware of any alternative to what he has become. He begins by killing his dog and ends by killing his mother (which seems to trouble him less). *The Hive* (165) offers snapshots of Madrid, lives devoid of hope or joy or significance, with sexual encounters the only candle in the darkness.

Cela, too, is a master of the apt phrase. "The boy has the face not of a person, but of a domestic animal, of a poor dirty beast, a perverted farmyard beast. ... His face has a beautiful candid stupidity, the expression of one who understands nothing of anything that happens." "With every day that passes Don Roque is more convinced that his wife is stupid." "When Don Fernando Cazuela searched for the murderer, he found his wife's lover hiding in the dirty linen basket." "Several dozens of girls are hoping— what are they hoping for, O God? Why do you let them be thus deceived?" "Dona Soledad's imagination is slow, motherly, and limited as a hen's flight."

Don Ricardo asks his girlfriend what her wine tastes like. Maribel takes a sip: "I think it tastes of wine." He feels sick to death of his girlfriend. The women look like "decent lasses from Normandy who had turned prostitutes to earn enough money for a wedding dress."

By the time he wrote his later novels, Cela had caught a fatal disease: writing to please professors of literature, critics, and the committee of the Nobel Prize (he won one). For example, *Boxwood* proudly proclaims that it has no plot. It contains cooking directions, whales, witches, mermaids, ghosts, and "the exquisite". It aims at matching the jumble that is life itself. It has no trouble living up to that standard.

Juan Marsé wrote two novels about what life was like under Franco in post-war Barcelona. *Lizard Tails* is a good novel with some nice passages. A woman defends her husband's political orthodoxy: "He is a member of the Devout Fraternity of the Bearers of the Body of Christ." But it shows symptoms of at least a mild case of the fatal disease. The narrator is an embryo, and the main character a boy who converses with both the embryo and a deceased brother. None of this is relevant to plot or character.

I expected that his next book would be narrated by an embryonic bat. In fact, *Shanghai Nights* (166) is beautifully written and coherent. Those who lost the civil war are based in France and conduct raids on Spanish territory. A few are still idealists, but most are marked forever by what they did and suffered in a lost cause, no longer believers but incapable of normality without belief, degenerating into personal betrayal of their former comrades. The only one who remains fully sane is a half-mad captain who circulates a petition against air pollution. His failure to get signatures symbolizes the hopelessness of the resistance to Franco, despite the fact that the Fascist regime casts a black pestilential cloud over Spain.

I have read Spanish novelists whose work is set post 1950s. Perhaps I had bad luck, but all were fatally infected. In Juan Goytisolo's *The Garden of Secrets*, twenty-eight storytellers are not content to tell stories, but question the nature of memory, history and myth. *Forbidden Territory and Realms of Strife* is an autobiography that spans much of Spanish history. Sadly, Goytisolo is aware that its style must be worthy of a great artist and succeeds in being pompous and pretentious. Carmen Martín Gaite won many prizes. Her *Living's the Strange Thing* strains for effect. It is cliché-ridden ("you're even prettier when you smile") and just plain bad. ("Where? Where?" asks a philosophical child. "Far away, beyond" is the profound answer.)

Javier Marías uses stream of consciousness, so ninety percent of his novels are mental essays on love and marriage, what is past is past, nothing that happens happens, or perhaps there never was anything, habit and law, death and "not-nowness", how few take the trouble to understand what is happening to their loved ones when they are asleep. *The Man of Feeling* is not quite as bad as his "greatest novel", *A Heart So White*. Both identify good writing with pointlessly long sentences and endless paragraphs: the flow of inspiration is too powerful to be stemmed by punctuation.

José Saramago's *Baltasar and Blimunda* is a story of love in an eighteenth-century Portugal still haunted by the Inquisition. I have not numbered it because I cannot recommend reading it to the end. It uses magic realism— that is, it combines a historical narrative with fantastic events. In this case, the plot is both fantastic (they fly about on an airplane) and thin. However, the early chapters recreate the time wonderfully: the awfulness of urban life; the omnipresence of religion combined with rampant hypocrisy; the army becoming dysfunctional; a corrupt church bureaucracy that makes the corrupt civil service a century later seem quite natural; hair-raising descriptions of both an auto-da-fé (heretic burning) and a bullfight. If you think bullfights are barbarous today, read this.

After the first nine chapters, there is one good section on how the religious mania of the Portuguese king could impact on the whole nation, benefiting a few and reducing thousands to forced labour. Other than this, there is no reason to keep going unless you have been captivated by the story. Part of Saramago's genius is that he does not number his chapters, so either count off nine of them as you go along, or multiply the total number of pages by 0.26 and stop there. *Baltasar and Blimunda* was published in 1982. Within a few years, this good writer had been totally corrupted by streams of consciousness, boring musings, and the compulsory long sentences. He cheats in that he prolongs sentences by using commas where most people would use periods. Perhaps that innovation was counted to his credit. He got the Nobel Prize in 1998, and some consider him the world's greatest living novelist.

In 1989, Saramago published *The History of the Siege of Lisbon*, about an event that took place in 1147 and foreshadowed the demise of the Moors. We do not get an account of the siege of Lisbon, but rather what might have happened if a fleet of Crusaders had not done what they did, namely come to the aid of the Christian forces. Saramago seems bored with historical recreation compared to a love story set in the present, and the two often dilute one another as paragraphs bounce back and forth between them. As for style, he begins with a ridiculous six-page sentence and it is all downhill from there on.

In this genre the French author Philippe Sollers has set a standard no one can hope to surpass. He wrote an entire novel, *Paradis*, using only one sentence—actually not even a sentence, but one continuous phrase that stops only because the book stops. This achievement ranks with going through a prolonged head cold without blowing your nose. The Nobel committee wanted to give him the prize, but never managed to complete the first sentence of its recommendation.

ITALY

By 1925, Mussolini had consolidated his brand of fascism in Italy. Ignazio Silone was a Communist whose brother was beaten to death in prison. After a visit to the USSR in 1927, he denounced Stalin and became a Democratic Socialist. His first novel, *Fontamara*, does not achieve maturity of style, but you may wish to read it as a historical document. It alerted millions to the realities of Mussolini's Italy. Silone describes a peasant village in which the new Fascist government, with the collusion of the church and the wealthy, renders the lot of the poor even more miserable than before. The hierarchy of privilege runs from God to the local prince (the dominant landowner) to the prince's thugs to the prince's guard dogs to the peasants, who are worth nothing at all.

Silone's *Bread and Wine* is more nuanced and readable, but not outstanding. In 1935, an idealistic opponent of Fascism returns to Italy disguised as a priest. His experiences convince him that only a network of honorable men sensitive to class injustice can be truly anti-totalitarian. They must not submit to the discipline imposed by organizations, whether the Communist Party or the Catholic church, both of which began as champions of the poor but have become rigid orthodoxies and agents of repression. To his credit, the honorable men and women do not enjoy happy endings. At one point, Silone's hero says that after he lost his Catholic faith he was tortured by the notion that good had no basis but rules supported by sanctions. This seemed to "destroy the distinction between good and evil". So the basic dilemma of the human condition arises for a fourth time.

Carlo Levi was arrested and banished to the southern town of Aliano for two years, 1935 and 1936. *Christ Stopped at Eboli* (167) tells of his work as a doctor amidst a desperate poverty rare in northern Italy. The divide between the prosperous north and the poorer south—the reverse of Britain—is a permanent feature of Italian life and politics. In 1941, Levi was imprisoned in Le Murate in Florence, to be released toward the end of the war after Mussolini was overthrown.

In September 1943, the Allies invaded Italy from the south. Behind German lines, members of the Italian Resistance movement became active; eventually almost

100,000 lost their lives in battle or concentration camps, or killed as collaborators by the Germans. Italo Calvino in *The Path to the Spiders' Nests* (168) aims at neither branding the Resistance fighters as criminals (as Fascists did), nor worshiping them as proletarian heroes (as Communists tended to do). His narrator is a young boy to whom crime seems natural and who has no heroes. The Resistance unit is composed of a few criminals, some people who are there only by chance, and men of conviction to whom communism means little more than a world where people will treat one another decently. Some are filled with hate; one just loves guns, and shoots cats when he cannot shoot people. The ending is quite moving.

After World War II, the Communist Party of Italy emerged as the most powerful communist party in the West, with about one-third of the popular vote. Frustrated by its failure to win power, partly because of United States' manipulation of the elections, its core members sustained ideological fervor, looking forward to the day of the revolution. This psychology was slowly undermined by postwar prosperity and the fate of the Soviet Union. In 1991, the party's leader stunned the faithful in Bologna with a speech in which he declared the end of communism, and the party was dissolved. Look back to Terzani's *Goodnight, Mister Lenin* (in which he describes the demise of the Soviet Union) and read the first chapter. Terzani's father was an Italian Communist who kept a "gun hidden in the wall". Terzani gives an excellent capsule account of the decline of revolutionary fervor among communists in the West.

In the 1962 preface to *Bread and Wine*, Silone remarks that he has made no concessions to recent literary fashions. The fatal disease afflicted not only Spain and Portugal but the continent as whole, which is why I recommend so few modern European novels. I should say that magic realism, unlike the contest to see who can write the longest sentence, or the contest to see who can write the most self-indulgent and pedestrian stream of consciousness, can be intelligent. Rather like a laboratory experiment, it can introduce some fresh factor or event into the world—such as the incapacity of anyone to lie—and astonish us with the consequences. H.G. Wells did this long before magic realism was heard of.

Stefano Benni's *Margherita Dolce Vita* has some charm, but the narrator is a teenage girl who makes six wisecracks a page and succeeds in being funny only about once every forty pages. The author loses control of the magical element. There is a family whose baleful influence is used to dramatize every dismal thing, from the media and consumerism to soulless architecture and environmental degradation, to the religious right and the minutemen, to a brutality that ends history and a precocity that abolishes age: "You have murdered the world's long childhood ... Those who survive will grow old in an instant."

Elena Ferrante, *The Days of Abandonment* (169) is about a woman of thirty-eight with two children whose husband leaves her. You are gripped by a nightmare that lasts for almost 188 pages. The new woman turns out to be a twenty-year-old blonde with whom her husband has been having an affair for five years. For some reason, this enrages her. Ferrante's second novel, *Troubling Love*, is not as good, but if Neapolitan men are really the kind of sexual predators she portrays it is a wonder all women do not carry mace.

SWEDEN AND NORWAY

August Strindberg's plays are set in the late nineteenth century. Strindberg disliked the military, the church, the monarchy, politicians, stingy publishers, incompetent reviewers, and the narrow-minded. He endorsed women's suffrage, but later denounced the emancipation of what he called "half-apes, mad, criminal, instinctively evil animals". During his sympathetic period, he wrote *Miss Julie* (170). A young woman's fiancé does not like being made to jump over a riding whip she holds at some height above the ground. She has not anticipated that he might, as a result, break off the engagement. She sleeps with a servant who has power over her because he is male and uninhibited by aristocratic values. He convinces her that the only way she can escape her lot is to kill herself.

Ingmar Bergman was a film director and writer who died only in 2007. His major themes were death, illness, betrayal and insanity—see his oeuvre (171): *The Seventh Seal, Smiles Of A Summer Night, Wild Strawberries,* and *All These Women.* Bergman is not always grim. *Smiles Of A Summer Night* is about people switching partners and is funny. The chief character in *Wild Strawberries* is easier to identify with than many of Bergman's protagonists. On a trip to receive an honorary degree, he relives his past life and often unhappy marriage. Critics did not like *All These Women* but I thought it very funny. A great musician is tempted to sell out to the demands of a music critic, who wants him to play a composition called "The Fish's Dream". His wife has concealed a gun and is prepared to shoot him if he does so.

Turning to Norway, Henrik Ibsen wrote some twenty-five plays. Three favorites are (172) *A Doll's House, An Enemy of the People,* and *Hedda Gabler.* In *A Doll's House,* Ibsen attacks nineteenth-century marriage; it is often called the first feminist play. *An Enemy of the People* is about a doctor who discovers that some baths, built at great expense to bring in tourists, have contaminated waters that cause serious illness. He is not popular.

Hedda Gabler has married to escape boredom. She certainly does. A writer thinks he has lost the manuscript of his greatest work. Rather than telling him he left it at her home, Hedda gives him a pistol to commit suicide. She hears that he has killed himself and is exalted because he has done something so beautiful and free. She then finds that he died accidentally in a brothel. For complex reasons, she is in danger of blackmail about the pistol. She ends the play by shooting herself in the temple. It may be beautiful but, given the element of compulsion, it was not free. I am filled with unspeakable disgust.

If you conclude that the Scandinavians have caught a case of the Russian soul from their large neighbor to the east, you may be correct.

A FEW BOOKS ON AFRICA

Write southern Africa has produced three Nobel Prize-winning novelists: Doris Lessing, John Coetzee and Nadine Gordimer. I have read two books by each. I found the last had a style so contrived as to be painful and the others merely competent. You may want to Google them and see if you have better luck. Alan Paton, *Cry, The Beloved Country* (173) is better, and shows the disintegration of traditional society, particularly as blacks drifted to the cities. It was published in 1948 on the eve of the introduction of apartheid, the cutting off of tribal areas from white South Africa by declaring them separate "nations". Worse was to come, with rigid segregation of the "races" in all areas of life and the declaration of interracial marriage as a criminal act. The South African government banned the book, and later on militants condemned its theme of reconciliation between the races. Fortunately, Nelson Mandela was not listening.

As for black Africa, like most in the West I tend to read about these countries only when they are in the news. Oddly, the writers I enjoy most are from the Igbo people of south-eastern Nigeria. This may not be such a bad thing: it is probably better to begin to learn about Africa with in-depth knowledge of a particular nation than a smattering of books from the whole continent.

Nigeria has 155 million people, more by far than any other African state. The Igbo are perhaps the most sophisticated African people, one of the many peoples in the world who are said to be the lost tribes of Israel. The British Israelites are split into two groups: one believes the British to be only two lost tribes; the other thinks they are all ten. Bertrand Russell said he read their literature and whenever he met one he always took the other side: "Much delightful argumentation was the result." Some even think the Irish are the lost tribes. But quoting a rabbi: "They didn't get that lost."

In *Things Fall Apart* (174), Chinua Achebe adopts an unobtrusive prose style that allows traditional Igbo culture in Nigeria to speak for itself. The section towards the end, when the missionaries begin to alter traditional society, came as a revelation to me in that I had never understood why it was so easy for them to prevail. Traditional society had alienated many whom Christianity said were equals in the sight of God: women who had twins (the women were accursed and the twins killed); outcasts; young men who found it difficult to live up to the macho role prescribed for males. Violence against the missionaries led to swift reprisals from the colonial government. To his credit, Achebe does not castigate the "humanization" that the missionaries brought.

Nigeria attained independence in 1960. From 1967 to 1970 there was a terrible civil war between the Muslim tribes of the north and the largely Christian Igbo of the south. This ushered in a period of military rule that ended only in 1999, and every election since then has been flawed as politicians use their thugs to intimidate. The West is censorious about the lack of democracy in Africa. Britain could have done more to prepare its colonies for independence. When it left Uganda, there was not one black with a responsible role in the civil service, and the highest-ranking in the military was a sergeant called Idi Amin. His regime set a standard for awfulness.

Achebe's *A Man of the People* (175) is set in the pre-civil war period. It introduces the dominant theme of modern Nigeria, the often heroic efforts of a few to secure free elections and freedom of the press. The composition of the society makes this an almost impossible task. The politicians are utterly corrupt and use hired thugs to intimidate their opponents. They are sometimes tolerated by the army, sometimes murdered by a general who wants to rule. Since each ruler feels threatened, each is brutal in repressing opposition.

The novel makes it clear why independence did not lead to something better. Initially, there were a few technocrats who wanted reasonably honest and competent rule, but they were easy to isolate as assimilated intellectuals who had lost their black roots. The masses do not resent corruption, so long as their lot is gradually ameliorated. They have no concept of rule for the common good, and think it natural that the officials are corrupt: "Would a sensible man spit out the juicy morsel that good fortune had placed in his mouth?" There are a few heroes in the press but others sell their front page to the highest bidder. The rulers see the press as just another group of swindlers, and an editor who criticizes them as no more than a personal enemy. They see the universities as hostile and are not reluctant to use compliant appointees and force to control them. The educated middle class who care about democracy are often Igbo and can be demonized because of tribe and religion.

Achebe adds a nice touch in that, while educated Nigerians much resent criticism from the West, they call someone "bush" as an insult, implying he or she is merely a primitive untouched by Western education.

Chimamanda Ngozi Adichie in *Half of a Yellow Sun* (176) tells the story of two sisters during the civil war. The religions implanted by the missionaries have sunk such deep roots that they divide the country, particularly as religion and tribe correspond. The Hausa and Yoruba (Islamic) are provoked by a coup that puts the Igbo (Christian) in charge of the federal government. This is followed by a counter-coup, after which Hausa and Yoruba slaughter every Igbo they can catch. The fact that Igbo are more educated and run businesses and shops puts them somewhat in the position of Jews in Europe. The Igbo secede to set up a state called Biafra, and are crushed in the civil war that follows.

Millions of Igbo were killed by war, army purges, starvation and pogroms. Britain supplied arms to the federal government and these may have been decisive. The stated reason was to discourage the break-up of African states. Britain's concern for the fate of Africa was touching: it also wanted unimpeded flow of oil from the area.

Adichie's earlier novel *Purple Hibiscus* (177) is about the post civil war period. There are graphic passages on the prisons, the universal need to bribe, and poverty. The book wavers now and then, but has much good writing, a good plot and good characters. An editor who tells the truth is eventually murdered. The owner of the paper is a principled man, a fanatic Catholic, a donor to all good causes, and physically brutal toward his family. He dies before we see whether he would continue to defy the government and be murdered in his turn.

His sister is a Catholic, also principled but sane. When she loses her post at the university because of her attempts to save it from political control, she and her family are forced to leave for America. It is sad to see history repeating itself and no message of hope is preached at the end.

Chinua Achebe's 1987 novel *Anthills of the Savannah* is also about post civil war Nigeria. Achebe abandons his earlier economical style for a florid one and this is a pity, but you may want to read the book for its content. It portrays the evolution of an unreflective but well-meaning man into a tyrant presiding over the decay of his nation. There is a nice bit of ambiguity at the end: two of the tyrant's old friends are killed but it is unclear whether he is to blame, or whether it is just chance. The tyrant is murdered by a general who is clearly going to be a much more brutal ruler; this casts a different light on his own insecurity, and the measures to which it led him.

The Belgian Congo (later Zaire and today the Democratic Republic of Congo) has had such a dreadful history that it has attracted the attention of several non-African novelists. Barbara Kingsolver's novel *The Poisonwood Bible* is about a fanatic missionary and his family who live through the 1960 struggle for independence. The wretchedness of the ensuing power struggle and the counterproductive interference of the United States are well portrayed, but Kingsolver's lengthy political sermons should not be taken at face value: Lumumba may have been a nicer man than Mobutu Sésé Seko, but it's not clear he would have done any better.

For a much better novel on the Congo, read V.S. Naipaul, *A Bend in the River* (178). The country is not named but the location is clear. The despair of those who are Westernized is caught in the words of a party boss: "We're all going to hell and every man knows that in his bones. ... Everyone wants to make his money and run away. But where?" In 1997, an insurgency that quickly led to the fall of Mobutu evolved into a war in which eight African nations and twenty-five armed groups fought over the Congo. The war killed more than five million of its sixty-eight million people and hostilities linger.

You should not assume the Congo is representative of all of tropical Africa: in recent years some African states have begun to show political stability and economic growth.

CHINA, JAPAN, INDIA AND
THE MIDDLE EAST

Geographically, New Zealand is part of Asia and this would be the logical place to list books from my adopted country. John Mulgan's *Man Alone*, Janet Frame's *Owls Do Cry*, and Maurice Gee's *Plumb* are all outstanding novels. However, since I must ignore smaller countries in favor of the big three, I will resist the tug of chauvinism. Thanks to the fact the West keeps creating mischief there, the Middle East gets a mention, and I will say something about the Jews and that Jewish heresy, Christianity. Both originated in the Middle East, and both have been rather influential.

CHINA

John Fairbank and Edwin Reischauer in *China: Tradition and Transformation* (179) tell in good prose China's story from her prehistory to the present. As they say, history is indispensable for understanding contemporary China, particularly since the Chinese see themselves through the eyes of history.

Jung Chang in *Wild Swans* (180) summarizes much of twentieth-century Chinese history. The author's grandmother was born in 1909 and became a concubine to a high-ranking warlord. After her wedding she did not see him for six years. Her daughter, the author's mother, was born in 1931, the year the Japanese invaded Manchuria and began a war of conquest that eventually gave them control over much of China. In 1946 the Japanese withdrew, and the Communists led by Mao Zedong began their struggle for power, culminating in victory in 1949. The author's mother joined the Communists and rose through the ranks to marry an officer. In 1966, when Mao began the horrible "Cultural Revolution", the author was a teenager. She joined the Red Guards but lost faith when her parents were tortured. In 1976 Mao died, and in 1978 she left China to study in Britain.

Wang Lan, *The Blue and the Black* is the pre-eminent best-seller among modern Chinese novels. It is a romance that follows the main character from resistance to the Japanese, through the governmental corruption that led to Mao's victory, to the flight of the defeated anti-Communists to Taiwan in 1949. Sadly it is a potboiler, pitched at the level of late adolescence.

Yu Hua, *The Past and the Punishments* (181) is a book of short stories, of which at least three are first-class. "Classical Love" is a haunting recreation of an old China in which, during periods of famine, people sold their children to restaurants to be butchered on the spot to provide fresh meat dishes. Thanks to Mao's agricultural policies, famine and cannibalism occurred in rural China 1959 to 1960. "1986" reflects on the Cultural Revolution twenty years after it occurred. When a woman's husband disappears, the youthful Red Guards are mystified: "We didn't torture him" (as they did most of their teachers). The terror of the time is recreated when a madman stalks the streets. "The Death of a Landlord" gives a more vivid impression of the brutality of the Japanese during their occupation of China than any statistics could: as they rape a sixty-three-year-old, they tell her they are helping her recover her youth.

Yiyun Li, *The Vagrants* (182) is a good novel about China in 1979, soon after Mao's death. Life for most is grim, grim, grim. A child pulls down wall posters to see if the paste is still fluid enough to eat. (There is some flour in it.) You can see why China's élite believes it must give the masses a share in the prosperity some urbanites today enjoy.

The characters are complex. For example, two young women are executed for dissent, but when one was a teenage Red Guard she had kicked a pregnant woman in the stomach. Provincial political leaders are in a frenzy when they hear of disputes over doctrine in Peking: how can they avoid being caught backing the losing side?

Wang Shuo, *Please Don't Call Me Human* (183) loses something in translation, and the send-ups of meetings and mass displays probably appeal to those who have had to sit through them. However, Wang Shuo also ridicules everything about Chinese culture, and many passages are screamingly funny. A sage steeped in ancient wisdom says:

"Practise moderation, be kind to your mother, don't kick dogs, stop on red, go on green" and so forth. An orator thinks the audience is cheering. They are actually shouting, "Go piss in a basin and look at your reflection." Although banned, Wang is said to be the most popular author among urban youth. If this is so, the lid cannot be kept on China for much longer. The élite is going to be swamped by a flood of cynicism and ridicule.

JAPAN

Edwin Reischauer and Albert Craig in *Japan: Tradition and Transformation* (184) are excellent on how Japan developed a culture different from any other. They explain why Japan was unique in beginning to adopt Western technology in the nineteenth century, culminating in what is today the second largest economy in the world. Michio Kitahara in *Children of the Sun: The Japanese and the Outside World* "psychoanalyzes" Japan since 1853, when the West forced entry. He argues that Japanese history is partially about the country's tendency to identify with a successful aggressor. Kitahara quotes a journalist writing just before World War I: "We admire Anglo-Saxon imperialism and we hope our imperialism does not differ from theirs." A noble objective.

Fumiko Enchi, *The Waiting Years* (185) is a family history from 1885 to 1920. A man of substance has a taste for fifteen-year-old girls and replaces them as they age.

His child bride, now twenty-four, recruits his first live-in concubine, followed by another, and eventually he has an affair with his son's bride. The wife is supposed to be consoled by the fact that her husband is so successful he can afford concubines. She struggles to salvage some human dignity and safeguard the welfare of her children, grandchildren, the concubines, whom she sees as victims, and in-laws. By the late 1920s attitudes are very different. In Jun'ichirō Tanizaki's *Some Prefer Nettles* (186), when a husband and wife grow apart, the husband encourages the wife to take on a lover and he patronizes a favorite geisha. But the tug of war between the old mores and the new freedoms paralyzes them, and, Hamlet-like, they find it impossible to make a clean break and start new lives.

A geisha is a prostitute educated to please men not only sexually but also by her appearance, deportment, conversation, and so forth. Arthur Golden's *Memoirs of a Geisha* describes the tradition in detail, but it is now in decline thanks to competition from its Western equivalent, the call girl.

Yukio Mishima wrote 273 books, including fifteen novels. *Runaway Horses* (187) portrays the psychology of a young man who plots to assassinate business leaders during the Depression of the 1930s, men who are corrupting Japan by their greed and disdain for the poor. Worst of all, they are the shock troops of Western influences that undermine spirituality, culminating in the cult of the Emperor. The young man espouses the samurai tradition, which dictates murder of the wicked, followed by ritual suicide: this purifies the self in that an honorable death is the only valid goal of life, and invites the nation to purge itself. You understand why fewer than 20,000 men out of an army of six million were captured alive during World War II. These Japanese were close relatives of Islamic fundamentalists who become suicide bombers. Mishima is posing the same question that today obsesses Islam: How much of what is best in a religious tradition can be salvaged in a modern industrial society?

Mishima admired the samurai tradition. He committed ritual suicide at the age of forty-five because he wanted to dictate the manner of his death, and because he had by then written his greatest books. This is not a case of the Russian soul. The Russian soul sees life as devoid of meaning, and death the only appropriate artistic response. The samurai sees life as infused with spirituality, and death a morally significant act that purges the self of all that is ignoble. How much of this tradition survives in twenty-first century Japan is debated. Cynics claim it lives on only in a martial arts video game called *Bushido*. Others argue that even Japanese businessmen follow the seven principles: honor, courage, filial piety, loyalty, respect for others, justice and honesty. If all of their business dealings are truly just and honest, there can be no doubt that Japan is unique.

The autobiographical novel *Confessions of a Mask* (188) reveals that Mishima suffered a dissonance between sexual desire and love: desire was focused on sadomasochistic fantasies about young men, but these were devoid of affection; love had a young woman as its object, but she aroused no lust. The plight of the woman who is ignorant of his lack of desire and therefore baffled by his behavior is very moving. Despite his tragic themes, Mishima injects humor. *Confessions* spans World War II. A father is reconciled to the fact that American bombs may kill his daughter, but appalled at the prospect her corpse may be found attired in slacks. *Runaway Horses* describes the end of a boring lecture: "There was the same feeling of relief with which one sees a frightfully squawking chicken suddenly breathe its last and become tranquil."

The Japan of today is thoroughly modernized, as popular novels show. Haruki Murakami's *Norwegian Wood* is a readable one. By 1968, when the book opens, Japanese students were like students everywhere: a lot of sex, liquor, introspection and angst. Films, music and women's magazines have been Americanized. On the other hand, do not expect Japan to be like America. Women suffer far more discrimination. Job ads specify gender, women tend to be treated as second-class employees when it comes to training, retention and promotion, and maternity leave is rare. There is even special female speech: women are expected to use certain deferential phrases, and different words for "I" and "you". Employees are taught the etiquette of gift-giving (you must not give the same gift to two Japanese of unequal rank) and how to bow appropriately.

Linking Japan, China and Britain, Kazuo Ishiguro's *When We Were Orphans* (189) is a masterpiece, although marred by the improbability of how the main character thinks and behaves towards the end. Just after 1900, two boys, one English and one Japanese, play together in Shanghai. The English boy's father works for a company in the opium trade, and his mother becomes estranged out of moral outrage. Opium-smoking is destroying China but England does not care because it is making money. It has even fought a war to force China to accept opium imported from India. The appalling hypocrisy of the day is underlined: the company forbids hiring locals because they may be corrupted by opium.

After Japan invades China in 1937, the English boy tries to find his parents, who have disappeared. His boyhood friend is now a soldier, totally brainwashed by Japanese nationalism, but still human. He says he has a son back in Japan who does not yet know how awful the world is—"he plays with his toys and his friends"—an innocent, just as these two men once were.

INDIA

After Salman Rushdie published *The Satanic Verses* in 1988, Ayatollah Khomeini of Iran called the book blasphemous and put a price on his head. Fortunately, the only assassin who actually tried to kill him killed himself when the bomb he was preparing exploded. *Midnight's Children* (190), which Rushdie published seven years earlier, uses magical realism intelligently. India attained independence at midnight on August 15, 1947. Saleem Sinai was born at exactly that moment and therefore has the gift of telepathy. All children born within the next hour have special powers. Saleem uses their telepathy to convene a conference of "midnight's children", thus accessing the religious and political diversity they represent. Sinai himself is Anglo-Indian Hindu but has been switched at birth and raised by Muslims.

During the period leading up to independence, it became clear that there would have to be two states, one Hindu (India) and one Muslim (Pakistan). Each of the many smaller states that existed in colonial India was supposed to choose, and the ensuing religious strife was terrible. Over twelve million people left their homes to get on the right side of the border, many of them slaughtered as they fled. No one has an exact figure for the number killed but half a million is a good guess. The book uses the fate of the Sinai family to capture the history of the period and events over the next thirty years, including the state of emergency from 1975 to 1977, declared by Indira Gandhi. Rushdie sees Gandhi as a potential tyrant consumed by the lust for power. Fortunately, after establishing a semi police state, she overestimated her popularity and allowed a free election: she was beaten in her home constituency.

For more on post-independence and post-partition India, read *A Suitable Boy* (191) by Vikram Seth. It is a huge novel of nearly 1500 pages, but you will get an almost encyclopedic knowledge of India as it was in the early 1950s, when it was about to hold its first election. Remarkably, elections have been relatively free ever since. Seth uses four families and a love story to discuss the antagonisms between Hindu and Muslim; how groups attuned to the new politics were relegating the hereditary princes to the dustbin of history; the changing status of women—at least of a few urbanized women; and caste.

To see how terrible caste still is in India, read Rohinton Mistry, *A Fine Balance* (192). It also covers the period between independence and the state of emergency, and culminates in the punitive castration of an untouchable who insulted a local landowner. Sadly, even if caste disappeared in India tomorrow, it has deposited attitudes that poison the country, just as the residue of class poisons Britain. I refer to the sense that it is simply vile to trouble those on top, particularly if the trouble is caused by their whining inferiors. The following is a paraphrase from the words of my friend, the distinguished scholar Ramesh Thakur:

Ruchika Girhotra was an aspiring fourteen-year-old tennis player in August 1990 when she was sexually molested by the president of the provincial tennis association, a senior police officer. On December 21, 2009, nineteen years later, the man was convicted of the offence, sentenced to six months imprisonment with a $250 fine, but granted bail pending an appeal. In the meantime, the girl had been expelled from her school, subjected to vilification and harassment, and committed suicide on December 28, 1993. Family members who pursued her case were repeatedly harassed and abused.

V.S. Naipaul, whose books on the West Indies, Guiana and Africa have been recommended earlier, has written a trilogy: *India: An Area of Darkness* (1964); *India: A Wounded Civilization* (1977); and *India: A Million Mutinies* (1989). All are excellent but I particularly enjoyed *India: A Wounded Civilization* (193). If you read it only, you should be aware that the deep pessimism of Naipaul's analysis is qualified in his final book. He sees signs that the notion of freedom is undermining some of the rigidity of caste.

THE MIDDLE EAST AND THE WANDERING JEWS

Naipaul has also written two books on Islam that have enraged much of the Islamic world. In *Among the Believers: An Islamic Journey* (194) he traces the rise of fundamentalism in Iran and Pakistan. One theme is undoubtedly valid: the tension between wanting, if only selectively, the technological advantages of Western civilization and rejecting those aspects of Western civilization, such as secularization, that make the technology possible. In *Beyond Belief: Islamic Excursions among the Converted Peoples* he revisits the same countries. He now emphasizes that the poor and oppressed have lost hope and see their government officials as either

indifferent or hostile. He also argues that religious hypocrisy prevails: men grow beards for job applications and
then cut them off.

There is one book that, more than any other, conveys
how much harm the West has done by denying the
Middle East its own history. We keep sending arms and
armies into the area, even though the record shows that
every intervention has left its people worse off than
before. Read Robert Fisk's *The Great War for Civilization:
The Conquest of the Middle East* (195). And weep.

Of all the peoples with roots in the Middle East, the
Jews have been the most influential because of their influence on the world's great religions: Christianity and Islam
were both founded by heretics from Judaism. I refer to Saint
Paul and Mohammed. Since Jesus was a Jew, it makes sense
to read Jewish historians if one has been raised a Christian.

Jewish historians make five points. First, Christ had
brothers and sisters, some older than he. You can still
salvage the Virgin Birth by giving Joseph a wife prior to
Mary: the brothers and sisters were the offspring of
the first wife, which makes them only half-brothers and
half-sisters. It is odd that none of the Gospels mentions
this non-trivial fact.

Second, the letter of James, Christ's brother (or half-
brother), makes no mention of either the Virgin Birth or
the resurrection. It refers to Christ as "our Lord" but seems
to speak of God as something separate. "Our Lord" may
mean merely "Our spiritual leader".

Third, Christ refers to Gentiles as dogs, which suggests he thought he had a message for Jews alone. James was clearly negative when Paul, who had never met Christ, began to convert Gentiles. Fourth, when, at the age of twelve, Christ lectured the rabbis in the temple, Mary left Jerusalem without him and after her return chastised him. You might think that, given the circumstances of his conception, she would think him rather special and notice his absence (good there were no assiduous social workers about in those days), and need no explanation for his preaching. Fifth, a number of Jewish prophets emerged from Galilee at that time and performed miracles.

The eminent Oxford scholar Géza Vermès has written several books about Jesus from a Jewish perspective. The most recent is *The Real Jesus: Then and Now* (196). Vermès sees Jesus as a holy man who did not think he was God or the Messiah. Rather, he believed he had a mission to warn the Jews that the coming of the Messiah was near, and that they must purify themselves, not merely by obeying the letter of the law but by having charity in their hearts. Vermès also sees Jesus as having an unmatched gift of parable, which would have enriched the Jewish tradition if only the Christian church had not emerged and made him the symbol of an institution that has persecuted Jews so savagely. Christian scholars challenge these conclusions, of course.

Paul Johnson, *A History of the Jews* (197) is excellent, particularly on how the Habiru (the word was originally a term of abuse applied to roving bands of destructive pastoralists) eventually became one people—the Hebrews, or Jews. He presents the foundation of Israel as a triumph, without much sense of its moral ambiguity. Chaim Potok wrote *Wanderings: History of the Jews*, and with a novelist's skill brings out the variety of Jewish life over the centuries. I did not think it quite as good as Johnson.

I have saved the best for last: Isaac Bashevis Singer. I loved every one of his eighteen novels. A few will be enough to excite you about the history of the Jews during their long sojourn in Eastern Europe. Singer's *The King of the Fields* (198) is about Poland when it was not yet Poland. (Originally "poland" was just a word meaning "land of the fields".) It records when the first Jews and first Christian missionaries (a bad day for the Jews) came to that area in the twilight of the Roman Empire. In *Satan in Goray*, Singer uses a small village to convey the psychology of Polish Jews in the fateful year, 1648. One-third of them had been killed by Cossacks, and this had prepared them to believe in Shabbetai Tzevi, a false messiah. He latter demoralized them when, under threat of death, he accepted Islam.

In *The Slave* (199), Singer again goes back to 1648. A man escapes from the farm on which he is a slave with his lover Wanda, the farmer's daughter. Since it was death to convert a Christian to Judaism, she must pretend to be mute so as not to give away her origins. There is a vivid picture of a Polish nobleman driven to despair by his skepticism. When Wanda dies in childbirth, she cannot help but cry out and her "recovery" of speech is taken for a miracle. You can imagine the intensity of the nobleman's reaction. Most days, I think it is the best novel I have ever read.

Singer's *The Family Moskat* (200), a panoramic view of Jews in Poland, all the way from 1815 to 1943 when the Nazis attacked the Warsaw ghetto, is as good as *War and Peace*. It created a furor in the New York Jewish community because it describes a double adultery that occurs on Yom Kippur, the holiest of Jewish holy days.

LEADING YOUR CHILDREN INTO THE MAGIC REALM

We live in the era of the "romantic mind". Things must be exciting to be worth doing. For some, the mere fact that something *would* be exciting if it were true is enough to make them believe it *is* true, whether it be the Loch Ness monster, the Bermuda Triangle, or the United Nations' plot to take over the world by pretending there is an environmental crisis. That kind of temperament is hopeless. But there is no harm in making the pursuit of truth exciting if we can.

A word to those of you who are, or will be, parents. Since I am an "expert" about the theory of intelligence, people often ask me how to raise the IQ of their children. I tell them they should not aim at anything so trivial. What they should want to give their children is a lively mind that has reached its full potential for enjoyment and understanding. Unfortunately, no one can give that to another person: the person must do it for themselves by reading and thinking. And there is no technique or trick that parents can use to make their child love reading.

Dutifully reading to them from an early age is a good start, and not exposing them to television until as late as you can is a worthwhile idea. Above all, do not use television as a childminder. Aside from having had their leisure time filled up with non-reading, your children, if they are average, will have seen 10,000 murders by the age of ten. They will be conditioned to expect the cheap fix of a spectacular event—a murder, rape, car chase or sex act—served up to them every few minutes on a platter. This gives them a mental clock unfriendly to reading: they lack the patience to allow a writer to construct character, atmosphere, moral dilemmas and plot through the use of words that take hours to absorb. Readers have to give something of themselves to a book, rather than just passively observe it.

Whatever you do is less likely to be as effective as surrounding them with people, including yourselves, who love reading and visibly take pleasure in it. Children are not stupid: they can tell the difference between a parent who reads to them as a chore and one who really wants to read. So my last piece of advice is what no one wants to hear: if you want your child to love reading, you must learn to love reading yourself. I hope this book will help you create a new self that your children will want to imitate.

I am now seventy-six and the magic realm of literature captivates me as much as it did when I was four. How I envy you, people with years of life left to explore a world as wide and fascinating as you care to make it. I hope I have convinced you that what you need to read to be acquainted with history and the world in which you live will give you much pleasure. These books will set your feet on the way to the kind of education no university offers. And just think: no fees, no classes to attend, no exams to take.

LIST OF WORKS

Works, both numbered and unnumbered, are listed in the order in which they appear in the text. Remember, the unnumbered are a mixed bag, some worth reading and some not. I also give the page or pages on which the book (or, in some cases, the film, play or poem) is discussed. The editions of books given are the most recent in paperback, or in hardback if there is no paperback edition. Many books have been published over the years in a variety of editions, and by a variety of publishers in different places. Many are also now available as eBooks and audio books. Consult your local library, or a physical or online bookstore, for more information.

page/s

1 C.L. Barber, *The Story of Language*: Pan Books, London, 1972. (First published 1964.) — 11

2 Hugh Lloyd-Jones (editor), *The Greek World*: Penguin, London, 1965. (First published 1962.) — 11

3 John Chadwick, *The Decipherment of Linear B*: Cambridge University Press, Cambridge, 1990. (First published 1958.) — 12

4 Alfred Hooper, *Makers of Mathematics:* Faber   12
   and Faber, London, 1961. (First published 1948.)

5 Arthur Koestler, *The Sleepwalkers: A History of*   13
   Man's Changing Vision of the Universe: Penguin,
   London, 1989. (First published 1959.)

6 Richard Westfall, *The Life of Isaac Newton:*   14
   Cambridge University Press, Cambridge, 1994.
   (First published 1993.)

7 Lisa Jardine, *The Curious Life of Robert Hooke:*   14
   The Man Who Measured London: HarperCollins,
   New York, 2005. (First published 2004.)

8 Jenny Uglow, *The Lunar Men: The Friends Who*   14
   Made the Future: Faber and Faber, London, 2002.
   Also published as *The Lunar Men: Five Friends*
   Whose Curiosity Changed the World: Farrar, Straus
   and Giroux, New York, 2003. (First published 2002.)

9 John Gribbin, *In Search of the Big Bang: The Life*   15
   and Death of the Universe: Penguin, London,
   1998. (First published 1986.)

10 John Gribbin, *The Universe: A Biography:*   15
    Penguin, London, 2008. (First published as
    The Origins of the Future: Ten Questions for the
    Next Ten Years: Yale University Press, 2006.)

11 David Bodanis, *E=mc²: A Biography of the*   16
    World's Most Famous Equation: Berkley, New York,
    2001. (First published 2000.)

12 Adrian Desmond, James Moore and Janet   16
Browne, *Charles Darwin*: Oxford University Press
USA, New York, 2007. (First published in *Oxford
Dictionary of National Biography*, 2004.)

13 Richard Dawkins, *The Blind Watchmaker*:   16
Penguin, London, 2006. (First published 1986.)

14 George Gaylord Simpson, *The Meaning of*   17
*Evolution: A Study of the History of Life and of
Its Significance for Man*: Yale University Press,
New Haven, 1967. (First published 1949.)

15 Julian Huxley, *Evolution in Action*: Harper &   17
Row, New York, 1966. (First published 1953.)

16 C.R. Hallpike, *How We Got Here: From Bows*   17
and Arrows to the Space Age: AuthorHouse UK,
Central Milton Keynes, 2008. (First published 2008.)

17 Jared Diamond, *The Rise and Fall of the Third*   17
*Chimpanzee: How Our Animal Heritage Affects
the Way We Live*: Vintage, New York, 1992. Also
published as *The Rise and Fall of the Third
Chimpanzee: Evolution and Human Life*, 2004, and
*The Third Chimpanzee: The Evolution and Future
of the Human Animal*: HarperCollins, New York,
2006. (First published 1992.)

18 Jared Diamond, *Collapse: How Societies Choose*   18
To Fail or Succeed: Penguin, New York, 2006.
(First published 2005.)

19   Calder Willingham, *The Gates of Hell*: Mayflower   19
Books, New York, 1970. (First published 1951.)

20   Terry Southern, *The Magic Christian*: Grove   19
Press, New York, 1996. (First published 1959.)

21   Donna Tartt, *The Secret History*: Vintage,   19
New York, 2004. (First published 1992.)

22   Tom Wolfe, *I Am Charlotte Simmons*: Picador,   20
New York, 2005. (First published 2004.)

23   Calder Willingham, *End as a Man*: Plume,   20
New York, 1986. (First published 1947.)

Gore Vidal, *Burr*: Vintage, New York, 2000.   20
(First published 1973.)

Gore Vidal, *1876*: Vintage, New York, 2000.   20
(First published 1976.)

Gore Vidal, *Empire*: Vintage, New York, 2000.   20
(First published 1987.)

Gore Vidal, *Hollywood*: Vintage, New York, 2000.   20
(First published 1990.)

Gore Vidal, *The Golden Age*: Vintage, New York,   20
2001. (First published 2000.)

24   Gore Vidal, *Lincoln*: Vintage, New York, 2000.   20
(First published 1984.)

Bruce Catton, *Mr Lincoln's Army*: Anchor Books,   20
New York, 1990. (First published 1951.)

Bruce Catton, *Glory Road*: Ace Books, New York,   20
1991. (First published 1952.)

25 Bruce Catton, *A Stillness at Appomattox*: Anchor   20
Books, New York, 1990. (First published 1953.)

Trilogy also published in one volume:
Bruce Catton, *Bruce Catton's Civil War:
Mr Lincoln's Army; Glory Road; A Stillness at
Appomattox*: Random House, New York, 1988.

26 Bruce Catton, *Bruce Catton's Civil War: The   20
Coming Fury; Terrible Swift Sword; Never Call
Retreat*: Phoenix Press, London, 2001.
(First published as Bruce Catton, *The Centennial
History of the Civil War*: Doubleday, New York,
1961–1965.)

27 Samuel Hopkins Adams, *Sunrise to Sunset*:   20
Bantam, New York, 1953. (First published 1950.)

28 Ray Ginger, *The Bending Cross: A Biography   21
of Eugene V. Debs*: Haymarket Books, Chicago,
2006. (First published 1949.)

The IWW, *I.W.W. Songs – To Fan the Flames   21
of Discontent: A Reprint of the Nineteenth Edition
(1923) of the Famous "Little Red Song Book"*:
Charles H. Kerr Publishing Company, Chicago, 2003.

29 E.L. Doctorow, *Ragtime*: Random House, New   22
York, 2007. (First published 1975.)

30 E.L. Doctorow, *Billy Bathgate*: Plume,   22
New York, 1998. (First published 1989.)

31 John Dos Passos, *U.S.A.: The 42nd Parallel; 1919;*   22
The Big Money: Library of America, New York, 1996.
(*The 42nd Parallel*, first published 1930; *1919*, first
published 1932; *The Big Money*, first published 1933.)

32 John Steinbeck, *The Grapes of Wrath*: Penguin,   22
New York, 2002. (First published 1939.)

John Ford (director), *The Grapes of Wrath*:   22
Twentieth Century Fox, Los Angeles.
(Film, released 1940.)

John Steinbeck, *Cannery Row*: Penguin,   23
New York, 2002. (First published 1945.)

John Steinbeck, *Tortilla Flat*: Penguin, New York,   23
1997. (First published 1935.)

33 Saul Bellow, *The Adventures of Augie March*:   23
Penguin, New York, 2006. (First published 1953.)

34 Tom Wolfe, *A Man in Full*: Dial Press, New York,   23
2001. (First published 1998.)

35 Joseph Heller, *Catch-22*: Simon & Schuster,   23
New York, 2004. (First published 1961.)

Joseph Heller, *Good as Gold*: Simon & Schuster,   24
New York, 2004. (First published 1979.)

36 Norman Mailer, *The Naked and the Dead*:   24
Picador, New York, 2000. (First published 1948.)

45 E.L. Doctorow, *Welcome to Hard Times*: Plume,   29
    New York 1996. (First published 1960.)

    Robert Altman (director), *McCabe & Mrs. Miller*:   29
    David Foster Productions, Hollywood.
    (Film, released 1971.)   29

46 Dorothy M. Johnson, *The Man Who Shot Liberty*   29
    Valance; A Man Called Horse; Hanging Tree;
    Lost Sister: Riverbend Publishing, Helena,
    Montana, 2005.

47 Oscar Handlin, *The Uprooted*: University of   31
    Pennsylvania Press, Philadelphia, 2002.
    (First published 1952.)

48 Cecil Woodham-Smith, *The Great Hunger:*   31
    Ireland 1845–1849: Penguin, London, 1991.
    (First published 1962.)

49 Noel Ignatiev, *How the Irish Became White*:   33
    Routledge, New York and Routledge, London,
    1995. (First published 1962.)

50 Betty Smith, *A Tree Grows in Brooklyn*:   33
    Harper, New York, 2005. (First published 1943.)

51 James T. Farrell, *Studs Lonigan: Young Lonigan;*   34
    The Young Manhood of Studs Lonigan; Judgment
    Day: University of Illinois Press, Chicago, 2003.
    (*Young Lonigan*, first published 1932; *The Young*
    Manhood of Studs Lonigan, first published 1934;
    Judgment Day, first published 1935.)

52 Mary McCarthy, *Memories of a Catholic Girlhood*:   34
Mariner Books, New York, 1972.
(First published 1957.)

53 Eugene O'Neill, *Long Day's Journey into Night*:   34
Yale University Press, New Haven, 2002.
(Play, first performed 1956.)

54 Irving Howe, *World of Our Fathers: The Journey*   34
of the East European Jews to America and the Life
They Found and Made: NYU Press, New York,
2005. (First published 1975.)

55 Chaim Potok, *The Chosen:* Ballantine Books,   34
New York, 1997. (First published 1967.)

56 Chaim Potok, *My Name is Asher Lev*: Anchor   34
Books, New York, 2003. (First published 1972.)

57 Tom Wolfe, *Radical Chic & Mau-Mauing the*   35
Flak Catchers: Picador, New York, 2009.
(First published 1970.)

58 Tom Wolfe, *The Bonfire of the Vanities*: Picador,   35
New York, 2008. (First published 1987.)

59 Sue Kaufman, *Diary of a Mad Housewife*:   35
Thunder's Mouth Press, New York, 2005.
(First published 1967.)

60 John Kennedy Toole, *A Confederacy of Dunces*:   35
Penguin, New York, 2000. (First published 1980.)

61 C. Vann Woodward, *The Strange Career of Jim*   36
Crow: Oxford University Press, New York, 2002.
(First published 1955.)

Abel Meeropol, "Strange Fruit": in David Margolick,   36
Strange Fruit: Billie Holiday, Cafe Society and an
Early Cry for Civil Rights: Payback Press,
Edinburgh, 2001. (Poem, written 1937; recorded
by Billie Holliday for Commodore Records, 1939.)

62 Lillian Smith, *Killers of the Dream*: W.W. Norton,   36
New York, 1994. (First published 1949.)

63 Martin Luther King Jr., *Stride Toward Freedom:*   36
The Montgomery Story: Beacon Press, Boston, 2010.
(First published 1958.)

Martin Luther King Jr., *Letter from the*   36
Birmingham Jail: HarperCollins, New York, 1994.
(First published 1963.)

64 Thomas Sowell, *Black Education: Myths and*   37
Tragedies: David McKay Company, Philadelphia,
1974.

James R. Flynn, *Where Have All the Liberals*   37, 76
Gone?: Cambridge University Press,
New York, 2008.

65 Thorstein Veblen, *The Theory of the Leisure Class:*   37
Oxford University Press, New York, 2008.
(First published 1899.)

76 Rebecca Goldstein, *The Mind-Body Problem*:   41
Penguin, New York, 1993. (First published 1983.)

77 F. Scott Fitzgerald, *The Great Gatsby*: Scribner,   42
New York, 1999. (First published 1925.)

Emily Dickinson, "I never saw a moor": in   42
The Collected Poems of Emily Dickinson: Barnes and
Noble, New York, 2003, and many other anthologies.
(Poem, first published 1865.)

James R. Flynn, "Journey down the South Island":   43
in *O God Who Has a Russian Soul: Poems about
New Zealand and its People*: Xlibris, Sydney, 2010.
(Poem, first published 2010.)

Edward Everett Hale, *The Man Without a   44
Country*: Hard Press, Lenox, Massachusetts,
2006. (Short story, first published 1863.)

78 Graham Greene, *Our Man in Havana*: Penguin,   47
London, 2007. (First published 1958.)

79 Jared Diamond, *Guns, Germs, and Steel: The Fates   47
of Human Societies*: W.W. Norton, New York, 1999.
(First published 1997.)

80 Jack London, "The Mexican": in Jack London,   49
Five Great Short Stories: Dover Publications, Mineola,
New York, 1992. (Short story, first published 1911.)

Jack London, *The Abysmal Brute*: Wildside Press,   49
Rockville, Maryland, 2007. (Short story, first
published 1911.)

Jack London, *The Game*: Wildside Press, Rockville,   49
Maryland, 2008. (Short story, first published 1911.)

Jack London, "A Piece of Steak": in *The Best Short*   49
Stories of Jack London: Wildside Press, Rockville,
Maryland, 2008. (Short story, first published 1909.)

Elia Kazan (director): *Viva Zapata!*: Twentieth   49
Century Fox, Los Angeles. (Film, released 1952.)

Carlos Fuentes, *The Old Gringo*: Farrar, Straus and   50
Giroux, New York, 2007. (First published 1985.)

Carlos Fuentes, *The Death of Artemio Cruz*:   50
Farrar, Straus and Giroux, New York, 2009.
(First published 1962.)

Carlos Fuentes, *The Years with Laura Díaz*:   50
Mariner Books, New York, 2001.

81 Oscar Lewis, *The Children of Sanchez*: Vintage,   50
New York, 1979. (First published 1961.)

82 Carlos Fuentes, *A New Time for Mexico*: University   50
of California Press, Berkeley and Los Angeles, 1997.
(First published 1994.)

83 Roland Joffé (director), *The Mission*: Warner   51
Brothers, Goldcrest Films International,
Kingsmere Productions and Enigma Productions.
(Film, released 1986.)

84 Thornton Wilder, *The Bridge of San Luis Rey*:   51
HarperCollins, New York, 2003.
(First published 1927.)

D.M. Loades, *Politics and Nation: England 1450–1660*: Wiley-Blackwell, Oxford, 1999. (First published 1974.) — 59

Claire Cross, *Church and People: England 1450–1660*: Wiley-Blackwell, Oxford, 1999. (First published 1976.) — 59

Malcolm Todd, *Roman Britain*: Wiley-Blackwell, Oxford, 2006. (First published 1981.) — 59

Michael T. Clanchy, *England and Its Rulers 1066–1307*: Wiley-Blackwell, Oxford, 2006. (First published 1983.) — 59

Michael Bentley, *Politics without Democracy: England 1815–1918*: Wiley-Blackwell, Oxford, 1999. (First published 1984.) — 59

Anthony Tuck, *Crown and Nobility: England 1272–1461*: Wiley-Blackwell, Oxford, 1999. (First published 1985.) — 59

94 Charles Dickens, *A Tale of Two Cities*: Penguin, London, 2007. (First published 1859.) — 59

95 Charles Dickens, *David Copperfield*: Penguin, London, 2007. (First published 1849.) — 59

Charles Dickens, *Great Expectations*: Penguin, London, 2007. (First published 1861.) — 59

96 Howard Spring, *Fame is the Spur*: House of Stratus, Cornwall, 2000. (First published 1940.) — 60

97 Cecil Woodham-Smith, *The Reason Why: The Story*   60
of the Fatal Charge of the Light Brigade: Penguin,
London, 1991. (First published 1953.)

98 Barbara W. Tuchman, *The Proud Tower: A Portrait*   61
of the World Before the War, 1890–1914: Ballantine
Books, New York, 1997. (First published 1966.)

99 Barbara W. Tuchman, *The Guns of August*: Ballantine   61
Books, New York, 1994. (First published 1966.)

100 R.H. Tawney, *The Acquisitive Society*: Dover   62
Publications, Mineola, New York, 2004.
(First published 1921.)

101 George Orwell, *The Road to Wigan Pier*: Penguin,   62
London, 2001. (First published 1937.)

102 Evelyn Waugh, *Decline and Fall*: Penguin,   62–64
London, 2003. (First published 1928.)

Evelyn Waugh, *Vile Bodies*: Penguin,   62
London, 2000. (First published 1930.)

Evelyn Waugh, *A Handful of Dust*: Penguin,   62
London, 2000. (First published 1934.)

Evelyn Waugh, *Scoop*: Penguin, London,   62
2003. (First published 1937.)

Evelyn Waugh, *Brideshead Revisited*: Penguin,   62
London, 2000. (First published 1944.)

Evelyn Waugh, *The Loved One*: Penguin,   62
London, 2000. (First published 1948.)

Heinrich Mann, *The Loyal Subject*: Continuum,   81
London, 1998. Also published as *Man of Straw*:
Penguin, London, 1992. (First published 1919.)

128 Thomas Mann, *Death in Venice*: HarperCollins,   82
New York, 2004. (First published 1912.)

Thomas Mann, *The Confessions of Felix Krull,*   82
Confidence Man: Vintage, New York, 1992.
(First published 1955.)

129 Thomas Mann, *The Magic Mountain*: Vintage,   82
New York, 1996. (First published 1924.)

130 Sebastian Haffner, *Defying Hitler: A Memoir*:   82
Picador New York, 2003. (First published 2000.)

131 Christopher Isherwood, *Goodbye to Berlin*: Vintage, 83
New York, 1989. Also published in *The Berlin Stories:*
The Last of Mr Norris and Goodbye to Berlin: New
Directions, New York, 2008. (First published 1939.)

132 Christopher Isherwood, *Mr Norris Changes Trains*:   83
Vintage, New York, 2001. (First published 1933.)

Henry Cornelius (director): *I Am A Camera*:   83
Romulus Films, London. (Film, released 1955.)

Bob Fosse (director): *Cabaret*: ABC Pictures,   83
New York. (Film, released 1972.)

133 Primo Levi, *If This is a Man / The Truce*: Abacus   83–84
Books, London, 2004. (*If This is a Man,* first
published 1958; *The Truce,* first published 1963.)

168 Italo Calvino, *The Path to the Spiders' Nests*: 113
HarperCollins, 2000. (First published 1947.)

Stefano Benni, *Margherita Dolce Vita*: Europa 114
Editions, New York, 2006. (First published 2005.)

169 Elena Ferrante, *The Days of Abandonment*: 115
Europa Editions, New York, 2005.
(First published 2002.)

Elena Ferrante, *Troubling Love*: Europa Editions, 115
New York, 2006. (First published 1999.)

170 August Strindberg, *Miss Julie*: Nick Hern Books, 115
London, 2005. (Play, first performed 1906.)

171 Ingmar Bergman (director), *Smiles Of A Summer* 116
Night: Svensk Filmindustri, Stockholm. (Film,
released 1955.)

Ingmar Bergman (director), *The Seventh Seal*: 116
Svensk Filmindustri, Stockholm. (Film, released 1957.)

Ingmar Bergman (director), *Wild Strawberries*: Svensk
Filmindustri, Stockholm. (Film, released 1957.) 116

Ingmar Bergman (director), *All These Women*: Svensk
Filmindustri, Stockholm. (Film, released 1964.) 116

172 Henrik Ibsen, *A Doll's House*: Dover Publications, 116
Mineola, New York, 1992. (Play, first performed 1879.)

Henrik Ibsen, *An Enemy of the People*: Dover 116
Publications, Mineola, New York, 1999.
(Play, first performed 1882.)

Maurice Gee, *Plumb*: Faber and Faber, London,   125
1982. (First published 1979.)

179 John K. Fairbank and Edwin O. Reischauer, *China:*   125
Tradition and Transformation: Houghton Mifflin,
Orlando, Florida, 1989. (First published 1978.)

180 Jung Chang, *Wild Swans: Three Daughters of China*: 125
Touchstone, New York, 2003. (First published 1991.)

Wang Lan, *The Blue and The Black*: Chinese   126
Materials Center, San Francisco, 1987.

181 Yu Hua, *The Past and the Punishments*: University 126
of Hawai'i Press, 1996.

182 Yiyun Li, *The Vagrants*: Random House, New   127
York, 2010. (First published 2009.)

183 Wang Shuo, *Please Don't Call Me Human*: Cheng   127
& Tsui, Boston, 2003. (First published 1989.)

184 Edwin O. Reischauer and Albert M. Craig: *Japan:*   128
Tradition and Transformation: Wadsworth Publishing,
Florence, Kentucky, 1989. (First published 1978.)

Michio Kitahara, *Children of the Sun: The Japanese* 128
and the Outside World: RoutledgeCurzon, London,
1995. (First published 1989.)

185 Fumiko Enchi, *The Waiting Years*: Kodansha   128
International, Tokyo, 2002. (First published 1971.)

186 Jun'ichirō Tanizaki, *Some Prefer Nettles*: Vintage, 129
New York, 1995. (First published 1929.)

194   V. S. Naipaul, *Among the Believers: An Islamic*   135
         Journey: Picador, New York, 2003. (First
         published 1981.)

         V.S. Naipaul, *Beyond Belief: Islamic Excursions*   135
         among the Converted Peoples: Vintage, New York,
         1999. (First published 1998.)

195   Robert Fisk, *The Great War for Civilisation*:   136
         The Conquest of the Middle East: Vintage, New York,
         2007. (First published 2005.)

196   Géza Vermès, *The Real Jesus: Then and Now*:   137
         Fortress Press, Minneapolis, 2010.
         (First published 2010.)

197   Paul Johnson, *A History of the Jews*: Weidenfeld   ·86, 137
         & Nicolson, London, 2001. (First published 1987.)

         Chaim Potok, *Wanderings: A History of the Jews*:   138
         Fawcett, New York, 1987. (First published 1978.)

198   Isaac Bashevis Singer, *The King of the Fields*:   138
         Farrar, Peter Straus and Giroux, New York, 2003.
         (First published 1988.)

         Isaac Bashevis Singer, *Satan in Goray*: Vintage,   138
         New York, 2000. (First published 1955.)

199   Isaac Bashevis Singer, *The Slave*: Penguin, London,   138
         1996. (First published 1962.)

200   Isaac Bashevis Singer, *The Family Moskat*:   138
         Farrar, Straus and Giroux, New York, 2007.
         (First published 1950.)

INDEX